Amazon SimpleDB: LITE

What is SimpleDB, how does it compare to relational databases, and how to get started?

Prabhakar Chaganti

Rich Helms

BIRMINGHAM - MUMBAI

Amazon SimpleDB: LITE

First published: April 2011

Production Reference: 1120411

Published by Packt Publishing Ltd.
32 Lincoln Road
Olton
Birmingham, B27 6PA, UK.

ISBN 978-1-849683-68-5

www.packtpub.com

Cover Image by Tina Negus (tina_manthorpe@sky.com)

Credits

Authors

Prabhakar Chaganti

Rich Helms

Reviewers

Deepak Anupalli

Anders Samuelsson

Ashley Tate

Acquisition Editor

James Lumsden

Technical Editor

Pallavi Kachare

Indexer

Rekha Nair

Production Coordinator

Alwin Roy

Shantanu Zagade

Cover Work

Alwin Roy

About the Authors

Prabhakar Chaganti is the founder and CTO of Ylastic, a startup that is building a single unifed interface to architect, manage, and monitor a user's entire AWS Cloud computing environment: EC2, S3, RDS, AutoScaling, ELB, Cloudwatch, SQS, and SimpleDB. He is the author of Xen Virtualization and GWT Java AJAX Programming, both by Packt Publishing, and is also the winner of the community choice award for the most innovative virtual appliance in the VMware Global Virtual Appliance Challenge. He hangs out on Twitter as `@pchaganti`.

"It's never been done" is a call to action for **Rich Helms**. He has built a career on breaking new ground in the computer field. He developed CARES (Computer Assisted Recovery Enhancement System) for the Metropolitan Toronto Police in Canada. CARES was the first computer system in the world for aging missing children. CARES has been internationally recognized as pioneering work in child aging. Rich has also created several generations of e-learning platforms including Learn it script and most recently Educate Press.

Rich can be reached at `http://webmasterinresidence.ca`. Rich is a seasoned software developer with over 30 years of experience. He spent 22 years in various positions at IBM including Chief Image Technology Architect. His credentials range from deep technical work (fve patents in hardware and software) to running multinational R&D.

About the Reviewers

Deepak Anupalli is Architect for the Server Engineering group at Pramati Technologies. He has deep insight into various Java/J2EE technologies. He represents Pramati on the EJB and JPA expert groups and has led the Java EE 5 certification effort of Pramati Server. He is currently leading the effort to build a standards-based web-scale Application server. He is a visiting faculty member with IIT-Hyderabad for a course on middleware and also speaks at various technology conferences. He holds a graduate degree in Computer Science and Engineering from National Institute of Technology (NIT Warangal, India).

Anders Samuelsson has over 25 years of experience in the computing industry. The main focus during this time has been with computer security. He currently works for Amazon.com with Amazon Web Services.

> I'd like to thank my wife Malena and my son Daniel and daughter Ida, for always standing by me and allowing me to spend time helping out with this book. I love you forever.

Ashley Tate is the founder of Coditate Software and the creator of Simple Savant, an advanced C# interface to SimpleDB. He is currently working on GridRoom, an application for collaborative sports-video review built on several Amazon Web Services, including SimpleDB. He lives near Atlanta with his wife and four children. You can find him online at http://blog.coditate.com.

Table of Contents

Preface

SimpleDB is a highly scalable, simple-to-use, and inexpensive database in the cloud from Amazon Web Services. But in order to use SimpleDB, you really have to change your mindset. This isn't a traditional relational database; in fact it's not relational at all. For developers who have experience working with relational databases, this may lead to misconceptions as to how SimpleDB works.

This short book is designed to bring Developer's up-to-speed on SimpleDB, and focuses on understanding what SimpleDB is, the differences when compared to a RDBMS, and the SimpleDB data model.

 This book is a LITE Edition of a longer book: *The Amazon SimpleDB Developer Guide*. This full book is 250 pages of SimpleDB goodness and covers more information including Data Types, Querying, Caching and more!

To find out more about upgrading to the full edition, visit www.packtpub.com/liteupgrade and log into your account for offers and help. If you don't have an account on PacktPub.com, visit today and set one up!

What this book covers

Chapter 1, *Getting to Know SimpleDB*, explores SimpleDB and the advantages of utilizing it to build web-scale applications.

Chapter 2, *Getting Started with SimpleDB*, moves on to set up an AWS account, enable SimpleDB service for the account, and install and set up libraries for Java, PHP, and Python. It also illustrates several SimpleDB operations using these libraries.

Chapter 3, *SimpleDB versus RDBMS*, sheds light on the differences between SimpleDB and a traditional RDBMS, as well as the pros and cons of using SimpleDB as the storage engine in your application.

Chapter 4, The SimpleDB Data Model, takes a detailed look at the SimpleDB data model and different methods for interacting with a domain, its items, and their attributes. It further talks about the domain metadata and reviews the various constraints imposed by SimpleDB on domains, items, and attributes.

What you need for this book

To get started with the book and try out the code samples included here you will need following software:

For Python:

- Python 2.5 (`http://python.org/download/`)
- Boto latest version (`http://code.google.com/p/boto/downloads/list`)

For Java:

- JDK6 latest version (`http://java.sun.com/javase/downloads/index.jsp`)
- Typica latest version (`http://typica.googlecode.com/files/typica-1.6.zip`)

For the PHP part:

- PHP with curl support enabled
- GeSHi (optional): If Generic Syntax Highlighter package is installed the PHP source will be formatted when displayed in the samples available free from `http://qbnz.com/highlighter/`

Who this book is for

If you are a developer wanting to build scalable, web-based database applications using SimpleDB, then this book is for you. You do not need to know anything about SimpleDB to read and learn from this book, and no basic knowledge is strictly necessary. This guide will help you to start from scratch and build advanced applications.

Conventions

In this book, you will find a number of styles of text that distinguish between different kinds of information. Here are some examples of these styles, and an explanation of their meaning.

Code words in text are shown as follows: "Typica provides a simple way to access the BoxUsage value along with the `RequestId`, when you query SimpleDB."

A block of code is set as follows:

```
public static void main(String[] args) {
    SimpleDB sdb = new SimpleDB(awsAccessId, awsSecretKey, true);
    try {
        ListDomainsResult domainsResult = sdb.listDomains();
        System.out.println("RequestID : "
            + domainsResult.getRequestId());
        System.out.println("Box Usage : "
            + domainsResult.getBoxUsage());
    } catch (SDBException ex) {
        System.out.println(ex.getMessage());
    }
}
```

When we wish to draw your attention to a particular part of a code block, the relevant lines or items are set in bold:

```
"Statement":[{
    "Effect":"Allow",
    "Action":"sdb:*",
    "Resource":"arn:aws:sdb:*:123456789012:domain/user*"
    "Condition":{
        "IpAddress":{
            "aws:SourceIp":"192.168.176.0/24"
        }
        "Bool":{
            "aws:SecureTransport":"true"
        }
    }
}
]
```

Any command-line input or output is written as follows:

```
memcached -p 12312 -d
```

New terms and **important words** are shown in bold. Words that you see on the screen, in menus or dialog boxes for example, appear in the text like this: "clicking the **Next** button moves you to the next screen".

Warnings or important notes appear in a box like this.

 Tips and tricks appear like this.

Reader feedback

Feedback from our readers is always welcome. Let us know what you think about this book—what you liked or may have disliked. Reader feedback is important for us to develop titles that you really get the most out of.

To send us general feedback, simply send an e-mail to feedback@packtpub.com, and mention the book title via the subject of your message.

If there is a book that you need and would like to see us publish, please send us a note in the **SUGGEST A TITLE** form on www.packtpub.com or e-mail suggest@packtpub.com.

If there is a topic that you have expertise in and you are interested in either writing or contributing to a book on, see our author guide on www.packtpub.com/authors.

Customer support

Now that you are the proud owner of a Packt book, we have a number of things to help you to get the most from your purchase.

 Downloading the example code for this book
You can download the example code files for all Packt books you have purchased from your account at http://www.PacktPub.com. If you purchased this book elsewhere, you can visit http://www.PacktPub.com/support and register to have the files e-mailed directly to you.

Errata

Although we have taken every care to ensure the accuracy of our content, mistakes do happen. If you find a mistake in one of our books—maybe a mistake in the text or the code—we would be grateful if you would report this to us. By doing so, you can save other readers from frustration and help us improve subsequent versions of this book. If you find any errata, please report them by visiting http://www.packtpub.com/support, selecting your book, clicking on the **errata submission form** link, and entering the details of your errata. Once your errata are verified, your submission will be accepted and the errata will be uploaded on our website, or added to any list of existing errata, under the Errata section of that title. Any existing errata can be viewed by selecting your title from http://www.packtpub.com/support.

Piracy

Piracy of copyright material on the Internet is an ongoing problem across all media. At Packt, we take the protection of our copyright and licenses very seriously. If you come across any illegal copies of our works, in any form, on the Internet, please provide us with the location address or web site name immediately so that we can pursue a remedy.

Please contact us at copyright@packtpub.com with a link to the suspected pirated material.

We appreciate your help in protecting our authors, and our ability to bring you valuable content.

Questions

You can contact us at questions@packtpub.com if you are having a problem with any aspect of the book, and we will do our best to address it.

1
Getting to Know SimpleDB

Most developers would describe a modern database as relational with stored procedures and cross-table functions such as join. So why would you use a database that has none of these capabilities? The answer is scalability.

This morning, CNN ran a story on your new web application. Yesterday you had 10 concurrent users, and now your site is viral with 50,000 users signing on. Which database will handle 50,000 concurrent users without a complex expensive cluster? The answer is SimpleDB.

Why SimpleDB?

- Scalability
- Pay only for your use
- Access from any web-based system
- No fixed schema

Challenges?

- New metaphor—write seldom, read many
- Eventual consistency

SimpleDB is one of the core Amazon Web Services, which include **Amazon Simple Storage Service (S3)** and **Amazon Elastic Compute Cloud (EC2)**. Amazon SimpleDB stores your structured data as key-value pairs in the **Amazon Web Services (AWS)** cloud and lets you run real-time queries against this data. You can scale it easily in response to increased load from your successful applications without the need for a costly cluster database server complex.

SimpleDB, as illustrated in the following diagram, is designed to be used either as an independent data storage component in your applications or in conjunction with some of the other services from Amazon's stable of Cloud Services, such as Amazon S3 and Amazon EC2.

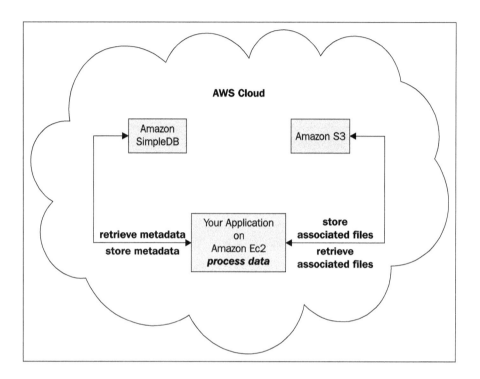

The biggest challenge in SimpleDB is learning to think in its unique metaphor. Like speaking a new language, you need to stop translating and start thinking in that language. Rather than thinking of SimpleDB as a database, approach it as a spreadsheet with some XML characteristics.

SimpleDB functionality can be accessed from almost any programming language (such as Python, Ruby, Java, PHP, Erlang, and Perl) using super simple HTTP-based requests. You can get started anytime you like, and you pay for it based on how much you use it. It is very different from a relational database, and takes a completely different approach toward storing and querying data. It follows the convention of **eventual consistency**. Think of it as a single master database for updates and a large collection of read database slaves. Any changes made to your data will need to be propagated across all the different copies. This can sometimes take a few seconds depending upon the system load at that time and network latency, which means that a consumer of your domain and data may not see the changes immediately. The changes will eventually be propagated throughout SimpleDB, but this is an important consideration you need to think about when designing your application.

Experimenting with SimpleDB

As SimpleDB is so different, it helps to have a tool for manipulating and exploring the database. When developing with a MySQL database, phpMyAdmin allows the developer to work directly on the database. SimpleDB has a similar free Firefox plugin called **sdbtool** (`http://code.google.com/p/sdbtool/`). Another Firefox plugin used in the more advanced examples is S3Fox (`http://www.s3fox.net/`) for administering the Amazon S3 storage. In this book, we cover several basic sample applications. We have also provided code to show each SimpleDB application using three languages: Java, PHP, and Python.

As access to SimpleDB can be from any site on the Web, the PHP samples can be downloaded and run directly from your site. To run any sample, an Amazon account is required. These samples let you explore most of the SimpleDB API, as well as some of the S3 API capabilities.

You can both download and try the PHP samples from `http://www.webmasterinresidence.ca/simpledb/`.

How does SimpleDB work?

The best way to wrap your head around the way SimpleDB works is to picture a spreadsheet that contains your structured data. For instance, a contact database that stores information on your customers can be represented in SimpleDB as follows:

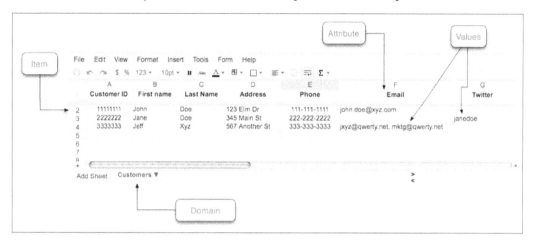

As SimpleDB is a different database metaphor, new terms have been introduced. The use of this new terminology by Amazon stresses that the traditional assumptions may not be valid.

Domain

The entire customers table will be represented as the domain **Customers**. Domains group similar data for your application, and you can have up to 100 domains per AWS account. If required, you can increase this limit further by filling out a form on the SimpleDB website. The data stored in these domains is retrieved by making queries against the specific domain. There is no concept of **joins** as in the relational database world; therefore, queries run within a specific domain and not across domains.

Item

Each customer is represented by a unique Customer ID. Items are similar to rows in a database table. Each item identifies a single object and contains data for that individual item as a number of key-value attributes. Each item is identified by a unique key or identifier, or in traditional terminology, the primary key. SimpleDB does not support the concept of auto-incrementing keys, and most people use a generated key such as the unix timestamp combined with the user identifier or something similar as the unique identifier for an item. You can have up to one billion items in each domain.

Attributes

Each customer item will have distinguishing characteristics that are represented by an attribute. A customer will have a name, a phone number, an address, and other such attributes, which are similar to the columns in a table in a database. SimpleDB even enables you to have different attributes for each item in a domain. This kind of schema independence lets you mix and match items within a domain to satisfy the needs of your application easily, while at the same time enables you to take advantage of the benefits of the automatic indexing provided by SimpleDB. If your company suddenly decides to start marketing using Twitter, you can simply add a new attribute to your customer domain for the customers who have a Twitter ID! In traditional database terminology, there is no need to add a new column to the table.

Values

Each customer attribute will be associated with a value, which is the same as a cell in a spreadsheet or the value of a column in a database. A relational database or a spreadsheet supports only a single value for each cell or column, while SimpleDB allows you to have multiple values for a single attribute. This lets you do things such as store multiple e-mail addresses for a customer while taking advantage of automatic indexing, without the need for you to manually create new and separate columns for each e-mail address, and then index each new column. In a relational DB, a separate table with a join would be used to store the multiple values. Unlike a delimited list in a character field, the multiple values are indexed, enabling quick searching.

It is a simple way of modeling your data, but at the same time, it is different from a relational database model that is familiar to most users. The following table compares SimpleDB components with a spreadsheet and a relational database:

Relational Database	Spreadsheet	SimpleDB
Table	Worksheet	Domain
Row	Row	Item
Column	Cell	Attribute
Value	Value	Value(s)

How do I interact with SimpleDB?

You interact with SimpleDB by making authenticated HTTP requests along with the desired parameters. There are several libraries available in different programming languages that encapsulate this entire process and make it even easier to interact with SimpleDB by removing some of the tedium of manually constructing the HTTP requests. The next chapter explores these libraries and the advantages provided by them.

There are three main types of actions that you will need to do when you are working with SimpleDB—create, modify, and retrieve information about your domains by using the following operations:

- CreateDomain: Create a new domain that contains your dataset.
- DeleteDomain: Delete an existing domain.
- ListDomains: List all the domains.
- DomainMetadata: Retrieve information that gives you a general picture of the domain and the items that are stored within it, such as:
    - The date and time the metadata was last updated
    - The number of all items in the domain
    - The number of attribute name/value pairs in the domain
    - The number of unique attribute names in the domain
    - The total size of all item names in the domain, in bytes
    - The total size of all attribute values, in bytes
    - The total size of all unique attribute names, in bytes

You can create or modify the data stored within your domains by using the following operations:

- PutAttributes: Create or update an item and its attributes. Items will automatically be indexed by SimpleDB as they are added.
- BatchPutAttributes: Create or update multiple attributes (up to 25) in a single call for improved overall throughput of bulk write operations.
- DeleteAttributes: Delete an item, an attribute, or an attribute value.

You can retrieve items that match your criteria from the dataset stored in your domains using the following operations:

- `GetAttributes`: Retrieve an item and all or a subset of its attributes and values matching your criteria.
- `Select`: Retrieve an item and all or a subset of its attributes and values matching your criteria, using the SELECT syntax that is popular in the SQL world.

The following diagram illustrates the different components of SimpleDB and the operations that can be used for interacting with them:

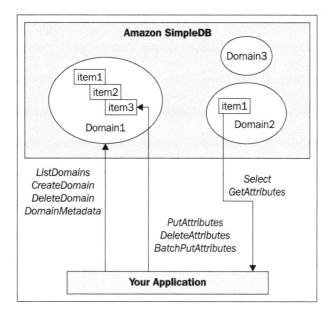

How is SimpleDB priced?

Amazon provides a free tier for SimpleDB along with pricing for usage above the free tier limit. The charges are based on the machine utilization of each SimpleDB request along with the amount of machine capacity that is utilized for completing the specified request normalized to the hourly capacity of a 1.7 GHz Xeon processor.

Free tier

As of the publication date of this book, there are no charges on the first 25 machine hours, 1 GB of data transfer, and 1 GB of storage that you consume every month. This is a significant amount of usage being provided for free for this limited time period by Amazon, and there are many kinds of applications that can operate entirely within this free tier. Pricing details are available at `http://aws.amazon.com/simpledb/`.

While a credit card is required to sign up, usage can be checked at any time with the Amazon Account Activity web page. Amazon estimates about 2,000,000 GET or SELECT API calls per month without any charge.

The pricing details might make it a bit daunting to figure out what your costs may be initially, but the free tier provided by Amazon goes a long way toward getting you more comfortable using the service and also putting SimpleDB through its paces without significant cost. There is also a nice calculator provided on the AWS site that is very helpful for computing the monthly usage costs for SimpleDB and the other Amazon web services. You can find the Amazon web services cost calculator at `http://calculator.s3.amazonaws.com/calc5.html`.

Why should I use SimpleDB?

You now have an overview of the service, and you are reasonably familiar with what SimpleDB can do. It is a great piece of technology that enables you to create scalable applications that are capable of using massive amounts of data, and you can put this power and simplicity to use in your own applications.

Make your applications simpler to architect

You can leverage SimpleDB in your applications to quickly add, edit, and retrieve data using a simple set of API calls. The well-thought-out API and simplicity of usage will make your applications easier to design, architect, and maintain in the long run, while removing the burdens of data modeling, index maintenance, and performance tuning.

Build flexibility into your applications

You no longer have to either know or pre-define every single piece of data that you will possibly "need to store" for your application. You expand your data set as you go and add the new attributes only when they are absolutely needed. SimpleDB enables you to do this easily, and even the indexing for these newly-added attributes is automatically handled behind the scenes without any need for your intervention.

Create high-performance web applications

High-performance web applications need the ability to store and retrieve data in a fast and efficient way. Amazon SimpleDB provides your applications with this ability while removing a lot of the administrative and maintenance complexities, leaving you free to focus on what's important to you — your application.

Take advantage of lower costs

You pay only for the SimpleDB resources that you actually consume, and you no longer need to lay out significant expenditures up front for database software licenses or even hardware. The capacity planning and handling of any spikes in load and traffic are automatically handled by Amazon, freeing valuable resources that can be deployed in other areas. SimpleDB pricing passes on to you the cost savings achieved by Amazon's economies of scale.

Scale your applications on demand

And last but most importantly, you can easily handle traffic and load spikes on your applications, as SimpleDB will be doing all of the heavy lifting and scaling for you. You can even handle the massive and tsunami-like increases in traffic that can result from being mentioned on the front page of Yahoo or Digg, or becoming a trendy topic on Twitter.

Architect for the cloud

SimpleDB is designed to integrate easily and work well with the other cloud services from Amazon such as Amazon EC2 and Amazon S3. This enables you to take full advantage of these other services and offload data processing and file storage needs to the cloud, while still using SimpleDB for your structured data storage needs. Web-scale computing for your application needs along with cost-effectiveness is easier thanks to these cloud services.

Summary

In this chapter, we explored SimpleDB and the advantages of utilizing it to build web-scale applications. In the next chapter, we will start interacting with SimpleDB, and getting familiar with creating and modifying datasets utilizing one of the widely available SimpleDB software libraries.

2
Getting Started with SimpleDB

In this chapter, we going to sign up for an AWS account, download and install the necessary libraries, and create little code snippets for exploring SimpleDB. We will introduce the libraries as well as the SimpleDB Firefox plugin for manipulating SimpleDB. We will also examine the two methods for accessing SimpleDB: SOAP and ReST. For PHP users we will introduce the PHP sample library. You can download and install the samples on your PHP5 server so that you can try the samples as you read about them.

Creating an AWS account

In order to start using SimpleDB, you will first need to sign up for an account with AWS.

Visit `http://aws.amazon.com/` and click on **Create an AWS Account**.

You can sign up either by using your e-mail address for an existing Amazon account, or by creating a completely new account. You may wish to have multiple accounts to separate billing for projects. This could make it easier for you to track billing for separate accounts. After a successful signup, navigate to the main AWS page — http://aws.amazon.com/, and click on the **Your Account** link at any time to view your account information and make any changes to it if needed.

Enabling SimpleDB service for AWS account

Once you have successfully set up an AWS account, you must follow these steps to enable the SimpleDB service for your account:

1. Log in to your AWS account.
2. Navigate to the SimpleDB home page — http://aws.amazon.com/ simpledb/.
3. Click on the **Sign Up For Amazon SimpleDB** button on the right side of the page.
4. Provide the requested credit card information and complete the signup process.

You have now successfully set up your AWS account and enabled it for SimpleDB.

All communication with SimpleDB or any of the Amazon web services must be through either the SOAP interface or the Query/ReST interface. The request messages sent through either of these interfaces is digitally signed by the sending user in order to ensure that the messages have not been tampered within transit, and that they really originate from the sending user. Requests that use the Query/ReST interface will use the access keys for signing the request, whereas requests to the SOAP interface will use the x.509 certificates.

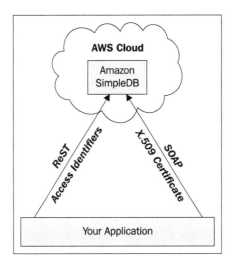

Your new AWS account is associated with the following items:

- A unique 12-digit AWS account number for identifying your account.

- AWS Access Credentials are used for the purpose of authenticating requests made by you through the ReST Request API to any of the web services provided by AWS. An initial set of keys is automatically generated for you by default. You can regenerate the Secret Access Key at any time if you like. Keep in mind that when you generate a new access key, all requests made using the old key will be rejected.

  - An Access Key ID identifies you as the person making requests to a web service.

  - A Secret Access Key is used to calculate the digital signature when you make requests to the web service.

  - Be careful with your Secret Access Key, as it provides full access to the account, including the ability to delete all of your data.

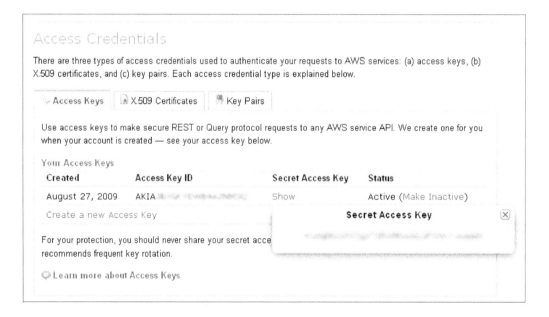

- All requests made to any of the web services provided by AWS using the SOAP protocol use the X.509 security certificate for authentication. There are no default certificates generated automatically for you by AWS. You must generate the certificate by clicking on the **Create a new Certificate** link, then download them to your computer and make them available to the machine that will be making requests to AWS.

      ° Public and private key for the x.509 certificate. You can either upload your own x.509 certificate if you already have one, or you can just generate a new certificate and then download it to your computer.

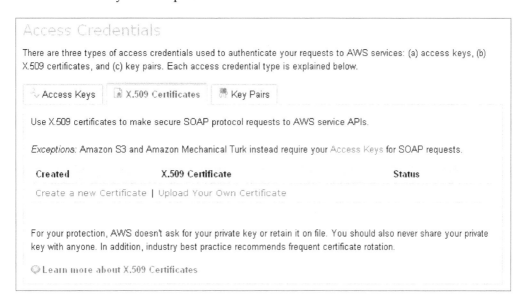

Query API and authentication

There are two interfaces to SimpleDB. The SOAP interface uses the SOAP protocol for the messages, while the ReST Requests uses HTTP requests with request parameters to describe the various SimpleDB methods and operations. In this book, we will be focusing on using the ReST Requests for talking to SimpleDB, as it is a much simpler protocol and utilizes straightforward HTTP-based requests and responses for communication, and the requests are sent to SimpleDB using either a HTTP GET or POST method.

The ReST Requests need to be authenticated in order to establish that they are originating from a valid SimpleDB user, and also for accounting and billing purposes. This authentication is performed using your access key identifiers. Every request to SimpleDB must contain a request signature calculated by constructing a string based on the Query API and then calculating an RFC 2104-compliant HMAC-SHA1 hash, using the Secret Access Key.

The basic steps in the authentication of a request by SimpleDB are:

- You construct a request to SimpleDB.

- You use your Secret Access Key to calculate the request signature, a Keyed-Hashing for **Message Authentication code (HMAC)** with an SHA1 hash function.

- You send the request data, the request signature, timestamp, and your Access Key ID to AWS.

- AWS uses the Access Key ID in the request to look up the associated Secret Access Key.

- AWS generates a request signature from the request data using the retrieved Secret Access Key and the same algorithm you used to calculate the signature in the request.

- If the signature generated by AWS matches the one you sent in the request, the request is considered to be authentic. If the signatures are different, the request is discarded, and AWS returns an error response. If the timestamp is older than 15 minutes, the request is rejected.

The procedure for constructing your requests is simple, but tedious and time consuming. This overview was intended to make you familiar with the entire process, but don't worry—you will not need to go through this laborious process every single time that you interact with SimpleDB. Instead, we will be leveraging one of the available libraries for communicating with SimpleDB, which encapsulates a lot of the repetitive stuff for us and makes it simple to dive straight into playing with and exploring SimpleDB!

SimpleDB libraries

There are libraries available for interacting with SimpleDB from a wide variety of languages. Most of these libraries provide support for all of the basic operations of SimpleDB. However, Amazon has been working hard to enhance and improve the functionality of SimpleDB, and as a result, they add new features frequently. You will want to leverage these new features as quickly as possible in your own applications. It is important that you select a library that has an active development cycle, so the new features are available fairly quickly after Amazon has released them. Another important consideration is the community around each library. An active community that uses the library ensures good quality and also provides a great way to get your questions answered. There are five libraries that meet all of these criteria:

- **Java Library for Amazon SimpleDB**: This is the official Java library provided by Amazon. In our experience, this library is a bit too verbose and requires a lot of boilerplate code.

- **Typica**: This is an open source Java library that provides access to all of the latest functionalities provided by SimpleDB. It is actively maintained and has a large community of users.

- **SDB-PHP and S3-PHP**: SDB-PHP is an open source PHP library that provides an easy ReST-based interface to Amazon's SimpleDB service (`http://sourceforge.net/projects/php-sdb/`), and S3-PHP is an open source PHP library to access S3-PHP (`http://undesigned.org.za/2007/10/22/amazon-s3-php-class`).

- **RightAWS**: An open source Ruby library for SimpleDB, which is quite popular with users who are building Ruby on Rails-based webapps that need SimpleDB functionality. It is actively maintained and has a large community of users.

- **Boto**: An open source Python library for SimpleDB. This is a comprehensive library that provides access to all of the SimpleDB features.

These are all great libraries, and they will be useful to you if your application is written in one of these languages. We will include samples in three of the languages—Java, PHP, and Python.

SDBtool — Firefox plugin

SDBtool is a Firefox plugin by Bizo Engineering for manipulating SimpleDB. As you go through the sample code, you can then view the results in the database. This is invaluable in both viewing results as well as updating or deleting data.

The program is a Firefox web browser (`http://www.mozilla.com/firefox/`) plugin. One of Firefox's key features is the ability to install plugins to expand the capabilities. Firefox is available for Microsoft Windows and Apple Mac OS X as well as Linux.

To install SDBtool, visit `http://code.google.com/p/SDBtool/` with a Firefox browser. Then click on the **Click here to install** link. Firefox will ask for a confirmation to install the plugin.

To start SDBtool, click on **Tools | SDB Tool** in the top menu.

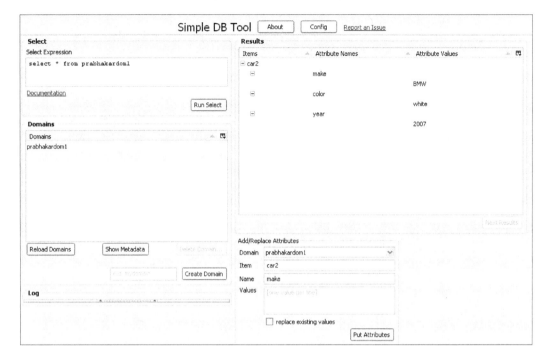

When SDBtool starts for the first time, it is necessary to configure your Access Keys. Click on the **Config** button and enter your Access Key and Secret Key. There is also a checkbox that sets if the tool can delete a domain. If you are working on a production database, it is wise to leave this unchecked.

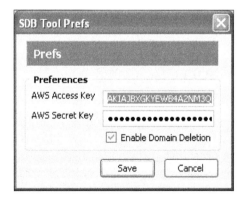

A connection to your SimpleDB database will open in a new browser tab. The list of available domains will be listed in the domain area.

The SDBtool screen is divided into four areas:

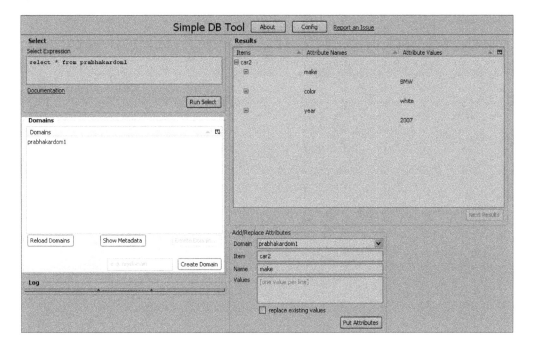

This area is used to create or display domains.

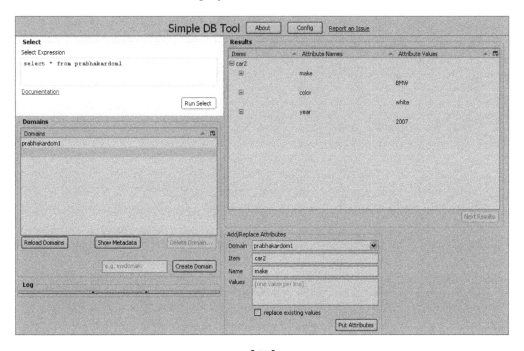

This area is used to write SQL queries.

Use the simple `select * from domain_name` to view all items in a domain.

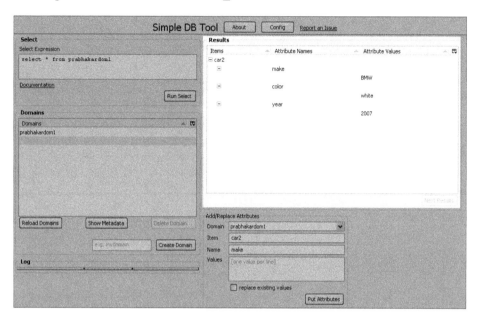

This area is used to display SQL query results.

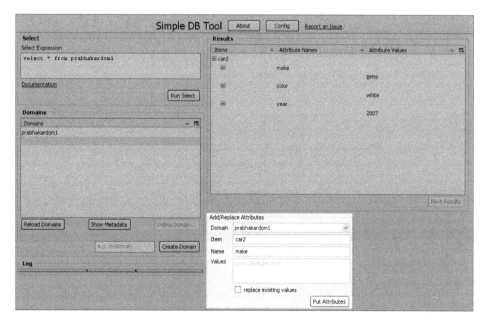

This area is used to add or replace attribute values.

Sample outline — performing basic operations

In this book, each sample set will begin with a sample outline. The sample goals, as well as common SimpleDB principles, will be introduced. Then the sample will break into three streams: Java, PHP, and Python.

The purpose of this sample is to introduce code snippets to create, list, and delete domains as well as create, query, and delete items.

 Each domain is a container for storing items. Any item that does not have any attributes is considered empty and is automatically deleted by SimpleDB. You can therefore have empty domains stored in SimpleDB, but not items with zero attributes. Each value is stored as a UTF-8 string in SimpleDB. This is an important consideration, and you need to be aware of it when storing and querying different data types, such as numbers or dates. You must convert their data into an appropriate string format, so that your queries against the data return expected results. The conversion of data adds a little bit of extra work on your application side, but it also provides you with the flexibility to enforce data ReSTrictions at your application layer without the need for the data store to enforce the constraints.

Basic operations with Java

Java is a very popular language used for building enterprise applications. In this section we will download **typica** and then use it for exploring SimpleDB.

Exploring SimpleDB with Java

Download **typica** from the project site at Google Code—`http://code.google.com/p/typica/`.

The latest version of **typica** at the time of writing this is 1.6. Download the ZIP file from the website. Unzip to the folder of your choice and add the `typica.jar` to your classpath. You also need some third-party libraries used by typica and can download each of these dependencies and add the corresponding JAR files to your classpath:

- `commons-logging` (`http://commons.apache.org/downloads/download_logging.cgi`)

- `JAXB` (`https://jaxb.dev.java.net/servlets/ProjectDocumentList?folderID=6746&expandFolder=6746&folderID=3952`)

- `commons-httpclient` (`http://hc.apache.org/downloads.cgi`)

- `commons-codec` (`http://commons.apache.org/downloads/download_codec.cgi`)

We are going to learn about and explore SimpleDB from Java by writing small snippets of Java code for interacting with it. Here is the skeleton of a Java class named **ExploreSdb** that contains a main method. We will add code to the main method, and you can run the class to see it in action from the console or in the IDE of your choice.

```
package simpledbbook;
public class ExploreSdb {
    public static void main(String[] args) {
        SimpleDB sdb = new SimpleDB(awsAccessId, awsSecretKey, true);
    }
}
```

In this class, we create a SimpleDB object from the class provided by typica. This will be our connection to Amazon SimpleDB and will be used for interacting with it. As we have discussed earlier, in order to use the API, we will need to specify the AWS keys. Typica lets you store the keys in a file named `aws.properties`, or you can explicitly provide them when you are creating a connection. In this chapter, we will use the explicit way. In each of the sections below, we will add snippets of code to the `main()` method.

Creating a domain with Java

A **SimpleDB domain** is a container for storing data, and is similar in concept to a table in a relational database. You create a domain by calling the `createDomain()` method and specifying a name for the domain.

```
public static void main(String[] args) {
    SimpleDB sdb = new SimpleDB(awsAccessId, awsSecretKey, true);
    try {
        Domain domain = sdb.createDomain("cars");
    } catch (SDBException ex) {
        System.out.println(ex.getMessage());
    }
}
```

Listing domains with Java

You can display a list of domains by calling the `listDomains()` method. This will return a list of domain objects.

```
public static void main(String[] args) {
    SimpleDB sdb = new SimpleDB(awsAccessId, awsSecretKey, true);
    try {
        ListDomainsResult domainsResult = sdb.listDomains();
        List<Domain> domains = domainsResult.getDomainList();
        for (Domain dom : domains) {
            System.out.println("Domain : " + dom.getName());
        }
    } catch (SDBException ex) {
        System.out.println(ex.getMessage());
    }
}
```

Manipulating items with Java

We will now add some items to our newly-created domain. You create an item and then specify its attributes as follows:

```
public static void main(String[] args) {
    SimpleDB sdb = new SimpleDB(awsAccessId, awsSecretKey, true);
    try {
        Domain domain = sdb.getDomain("cars");
        Item item = domain.getItem("car1");
        List<ItemAttribute> list = new ArrayList<ItemAttribute>();
        list.add(new ItemAttribute("make", "BMW", false));
```

```
                list.add(new ItemAttribute("color", "grey", false));
                list.add(new ItemAttribute("year", "2008", false));
                list.add(new ItemAttribute("desc", "Sedan", false));
                list.add(new ItemAttribute("model", "530i", false));
                item.putAttributes(list);

                item = domain.getItem("car2");
                list = new ArrayList<ItemAttribute>();
                list.add(new ItemAttribute("make", "BMW", false));
                list.add(new ItemAttribute("color", "white", false));
                list.add(new ItemAttribute("year", "2007", false));
                list.add(new ItemAttribute("desc", "Sports Utility Vehicle",
                                              false));
                list.add(new ItemAttribute("model", "X5", false));
                item.putAttributes(list);
        } catch (SDBException ex) {
            System.out.println(ex.getMessage());
        }
    }
}
```

Now retrieve the items from the domain by using a simple SELECT query.

```
    public static void main(String[] args) {
        SimpleDB sdb = new SimpleDB(awsAccessId, awsSecretKey, true);
        try {
            Domain domain = sdb.getDomain("cars");
            String queryString = "SELECT * FROM `cars`";
                int itemCount = 0;
                String nextToken = null;
                do {
                    QueryWithAttributesResult queryResults =
                        domain.selectItems(queryString, nextToken);
                    Map<String, List<ItemAttribute>> items =
                        queryResults.getItems();
                    for (String id : items.keySet()) {
                        System.out.println("Item : " + id);
                        for (ItemAttribute attr : items.get(id)) {
                            System.out.println(attr.getName() + " = "
                            + attr.getValue());
                        }
                        itemCount++;
                    }
                    nextToken = queryResults.getNextToken();
                } while (nextToken != null && !nextToken
                    .trim().equals(""));
```

```
    } catch (SDBException ex) {
        System.out.println(ex.getMessage());
    }
}
```

You can retrieve an individual item and its attributes by specifying the item name.

```
public static void main(String[] args) {
    SimpleDB sdb = new SimpleDB(awsAccessId, awsSecretKey, true);
    try {
        Domain domain = sdb.getDomain("cars");
        Item car1 = domain.getItem("car1");
        List<ItemAttribute> itemAttrs = car1.getAttributes();
        for (ItemAttribute attr : itemAttrs) {
            System.out.println(attr.getName()
            + " = " + attr.getValue());
        }
    } catch (SDBException ex) {
        System.out.println(ex.getMessage());
    }
}
```

Deleting a domain with Java

Finally, you can delete a domain by specifying its name. Once you delete a domain, the data is gone forever. So use caution when deleting a domain!

```
public static void main(String[] args) {
    SimpleDB sdb = new SimpleDB(awsAccessId, awsSecretKey, true);
    try {
        sdb.deleteDomain("cars");
    } catch (SDBException ex) {
        System.out.println(ex.getMessage());
    }
}
```

Basic operations with PHP

PHP is a popular scripting language for writing web applications. Many of the most popular open source applications such as WordPress are written with PHP. There are several SimpleDB APIs available. The PHP samples are based on an API written by Dan Myers. This program is easy to understand, use, and expand. Rich Helms has expanded the API and provided samples for this book.

All of the sample code can be downloaded and run from your site, or executed from our site, with your Access Keys to your SimpleDB. Note that the user interface in these samples is very basic. The focus is on illustrating the SimpleDB interface.

Exploring SimpleDB with PHP

Rich Helms: "When I wrote my first SimpleDB PHP program, I struggled to find a working sample to build on. After a number of APIs, I found Dan Myers' SDB-PHP. The entire API was in one file and simple to understand. Working with Dan, I expanded the API to provide complete SimpleDB functionality including data normalization. When I needed a PHP S3 API for backup/ReSTore of SimpleDB, I used S3-PHP by Donovan Schonknecht. SDB-PHP was based on S3-PHP".

Visit `http://www.webmasterinresidence.ca/simpledb/` to download the PHP sample package, which has the sample programs discussed in this book. All programs are complete and can be run unaltered on your server. The samples use PHP 5.

The menu (`index.php`) provides access to all samples. When a program is run, the source is shown below in a box. If the free package **Generic Syntax Highlighter (GeSHi)** is installed, the source will be formatted when displayed. To get GeSHi, go to `http://qbnz.com/highlighter/`.

SimpleDB PHP Sample Programs

Key/Secret Key
1. Set your key/secret key for the session
2. Destroy your key/secret session keys

Domains
3. List Domains and Domain Metadata
4. Create Sample domain 'car-s'
5. Delete Sample domain 'car-s'

Add Items
6. Create Multiple Records One at a Time in car-s
7. Create Multiple Records with batchPutAttributes in car-s

List Items
8. List All Sample Records in car-s
9. List All Sample Records with a NextToken car-s

Delete Items/Attributes
10. Delete 'car1' item from 'car-s'
11. Delete 'car3' item 'year' and one 'color' from 'car-s'

Data Normalization
12. Encode/Decode Numbers
13. Encode/Decode Dates
14. Encode/Decode Boolean
15. Encode/Decode Base64

Select
16. Create Songs Domain with Sample Items
17. Select Year='1985' from Songs
18. Try SQL Queries
19. Query all attributes for '112222222' Item
20. Delete domain 'songs'

Backup
21. Backup a Domain
22. Restore a Domain

S3
23. Upload MP3 Song to S3

API Code
24. Display 'sdb.php' and 'config.inc.php'
25. Display 'S3.php'

Download source files

Rich Helms rich@webmasterinresidence.ca

Source - index.php

```php
<?php require_once('config.inc.php'); ?>
<html><title>SimpleDB PHP Samples</title><body><h3>SimpleDB PHP Sample Programs</h3>

<ol>
<strong>Key/Secret Key</strong>
<li><a href=setkeys.php>Set your key/secret key for the session</a></li>
```

The samples are structured into groups: entering your Access Keys, domains, items, and attributes; data normalization, select, and S3; and backing up SimpleDB into S3. As you go through the programs, use the Firefox SDBtool plugin to examine the database and see the results.

Select the first menu item to set the keys.

Set SimpleDB Keys

Keys saved Return to Menu

Key: AKIA ⬚⬚⬚⬚⬚⬚⬚⬚⬚⬚⬚⬚⬚⬚⬚⬚⬚⬚⬚⬚⬚⬚⬚⬚

Secret Key: ●●

[Set Keys for this session]

The keys are stored in two PHP session variables.

The Key and Secret Key values are stored in two session variables. Program `config.inc.php` reads the session variables to set two defined keys: `awsAccessKey` and `awsSecretKey`. If you are downloading and running the source from your site, you can just define the keys and avoid the session variables. Using session variables enables you to try the code at my location and still talk to your SimpleDB without me having access to your keys.

```
require_once('config.inc.php');
if (!empty($_POST["key"])) {
    $_SESSION['key'] = $_POST["key"];
}
if (!empty($_POST["secretkey"])) {
    $_SESSION['secretkey'] = $_POST["secretkey"];
}
```

The program calls itself passing the value of the input fields.

```
session_start();
if (!empty($_SESSION['key'])) $key = $_SESSION['key'];
if (!empty($_SESSION['secretkey'])) $secretkey =
    $_SESSION['secretkey'];
// if your own installation, just replace $key and $secretkey
//   with your values
if (!defined('awsAccessKey')) define('awsAccessKey', $key);
if (!defined('awsSecretKey')) define('awsSecretKey', $secretkey);
```

When the second menu item is selected, the session variables are destroyed.

```
require_once('config.inc.php');
session_destroy();
```

To access SimpleDB, first we create a connection. File `sdb.php` has the API functions.

```
require_once('config.inc.php');
if (!class_exists('SimpleDB')) require_once('sdb.php');
$sdb = new SimpleDB(awsAccessKey, awsSecretKey);
```

Creating a domain with PHP

A **SimpleDB domain** is a container for storing data, and is similar in concept to a table in a relational database. Once the connection to SimpleDB is made, to create a domain, call the `createDomain` function passing the domain name.

```
$domain = "cars";
$sdb->createDomain($domain);
```

Listing domains with PHP

To display the domains, make a connection, and then call `listDomains`. The function returns an array of values. Retrieving a list of all our domains will return an array of domain names. In addition to the domain name (`$domainname`), the function `domainMetadata` is called to return the information on the domain, such as when the domain was created, the number of items and attributes, and the sizes of attribute names and values.

```
$domainList = $sdb->listDomains();
if ($domainList) {
    foreach ($domainList as $domainName) {
        echo "Domain: <b>$domainName</b><br>";
        print_r($sdb->domainMetadata($domainName));
    }
}
```

Manipulating items with PHP

This sample creates two items in the most basic manner of one at a time. This sample also only deals with a single value for each attribute. Once the connection is made, three variables are prepared. The item name (`$item_name`) is the primary key of the item. An array is built with attribute names and values. Then the three variables are passed to the `putAttributes` function.

```
$domain = "cars";
$item_name = "car1";
$putAttributesRequest["make"] = array("value" => "BMW");
$putAttributesRequest["color"] = array("value" => "grey");
```

```
$putAttributesRequest["year"] = array("value" => "2008");
$putAttributesRequest["desc"] = array("value" => "Sedan");
$putAttributesRequest["model"] = array("value" => "530i");

$sdb->putAttributes($domain,$item_name,$putAttributesRequest);

$item_name = "car2";
$putAttributesRequest["make"] = array("value" => "BMW");
$putAttributesRequest["color"] = array("value" => "white");
$putAttributesRequest["year"] = array("value" => "2007");
$putAttributesRequest["desc"] = array("value" =>
    "Sports Utility Vehicle");
$putAttributesRequest["model"] = array("value" => "X5");

$sdb->putAttributes($domain,$item_name,$putAttributesRequest);
```

You can query for items within a domain by specifying the attribute and value to match. The SELECT syntax is a new addition to SimpleDB and allows searching your domains using simple SQL-like query expressions. The previous version of SimpleDB supported only a query-style syntax that is now being deprecated in favor of the simpler and easier-to-use SELECT expressions. Now that the items are created in the cars domain, we can list them as follows:

```
$domain = "cars";
print_r($sdb->select($domain,"select * from $domain"));
```

To retrieve a select item by the attribute value, you can use the following:

```
$domain = "cars";
$item_make = "BMW";
print_r($sdb->select($domain,"select * from $domain where
                            make='$item_make'"));
```

To retrieve a specific item by the item name, you can use the following:

```
$domain = "cars";
$item_name = "car1";
print_r($sdb->getAttributes($domain,$item_name));
```

To delete a specific item, you can use the following:

```
$domain = "cars";
$item_name = "car1";
$sdb->deleteAttributes($domain,$item_name);
```

To delete specific attribute values, but leave the item, use the following lines of code:

 Note: if all attributes are deleted, then the item is deleted.

```
$domain = "cars";
$item_name = "car2";
$deleteAttributesRequest = array("make", "color", "year",
    "desc", "model");
$deleteAttributesRequest["desc"] = "Sports Utility Vehicle";
$deleteAttributesRequest["model"] = "X5";
$sdb->deleteAttributes($domain,$item_name,$deleteAttributesRequest);
```

This code deletes the `desc` and `model` attributes from the `car2` item.

Deleting a domain with PHP

Finally, you delete a domain by specifying its name. Once you delete a domain, the data is gone forever. So use caution when deleting a domain!

```
$domain = "cars";
$sdb->deleteDomain($domain);
```

Basic operations with Python

Prabhakar Chaganti: "My personal preference is for the Python library—boto, which has a very nicely designed interface and a great community of users".

Python is an elegant, open source, object-oriented programming language that is great for rapid application development. Python is a stable, mature language that has been around for quite a long period of time, and is widely used across many of the industries and in a large variety of applications. It comes with an interactive console that can be used for quick evaluation of code snippets and makes experimentation with new APIs very easy. Python is a dynamically-typed language that gives you the power to program in a compact and concise manner. There is no such verbosity that is associated with a statically-typed language such as Java. It will be much easier to grasp the concepts of SimpleDB without drowning in a lot of lines of repetitive code. Most importantly, Python will bring fun back into your programming!

Introducing boto

Boto is an open source Python library for communicating with all of the Amazon web services, including SimpleDB. It was originally conceived by Mitch Garnaat and is currently maintained and enhanced by him and a community of developers. It is by far Prabhakar's favorite library for interacting with AWS, and is very easy to use. Boto works with most recent versions of Python, but please make sure that you are using at least a 2.5.x version of Python. Do not use Python 3.x, as boto will not currently work with it. All versions of Linux usually ship with Python, but if you are running on Windows or Mac OS X, you will need to download and install a version of Python for your platform from `http://python.org/download/`. There are installers available for Windows and Mac OS X, and the installation process is as simple as downloading the correct file and then double-clicking on the file. If you have Python already installed, you can easily verify the version from a terminal window.

```
$ python
```

```
Python 2.5.1 (r251:54863, Feb  6 2009, 19:02:12)
[GCC 4.0.1 (Apple Inc. build 5465)] on darwin
Type "help", "copyright", "credits" or "license" for more information.
>>>
```

You will need a copy of the `setuptools` package before you can install boto. Download the latest version for your platform from the **setuptools** page— `http://pypi.python.org/pypi/setuptools`. If you are on Windows, just run the downloaded EXE file. If you are running on Linux, use your existing package manager to install it. For instance, on Ubuntu, you can install `setuptools` using the apt package manager.

```
$ sudo apt-get install python-setuptools
```

Download boto from the project page at `http://code.google.com/p/boto/`. The latest version at the time of writing this chapter is boto-1.8d, and is provided as a g-zipped distribution that needs to be un-archived after download.

```
$ tar -zxvf boto-1.8d.tar.gz
```

This will create a folder named `boto-1.8d` and un-archive all the files. Now change into this new folder and run the install script to install boto.

```
$ sudo python setup.py install
```

This will byte-compile and install boto into your system. Before you use boto, you must set up your environment so that boto can find your AWS Access key identifiers. You can get your Access Keys from your AWS account page. Set up two environment variables to point to each of the keys.

```
$ export AWS_ACCESS_KEY_ID=Your_AWS_Access_Key_ID
```

```
$ export AWS_SECRET_ACCESS_KEY=Your_AWS_Secret_Access_Key
```

You can now check if boto is correctly installed and available by using the Python Interpreter and importing the library. If you don't have any errors, then you have boto installed correctly.

```
$ python
Python 2.5.1 (r251:54863, Feb  6 2009, 19:02:12)
[GCC 4.0.1 (Apple Inc. build 5465)] on darwin
Type "help", "copyright", "credits" or "license" for more information.
>>>
>>> import boto
```

Exploring SimpleDB with Python

We will now use the installed and configured boto library to run some basic operations in SimpleDB using the Python console. This will quickly get you familiar with both boto and various SimpleDB operations. Boto will use the environment variable for the Access Keys that we set up in the previous section for connecting to SimpleDB.

We first create a connection to SimpleDB.

```
>>> import boto
>>> sdb_connection = boto.connect_sdb()
>>>
```

Boto is using the AWS Access Keys we previously set up in the environmental variables in this case. You can also explicitly specify the Access Keys on creation.

```
>>> import boto
>>> sdb_connection = boto.connect_sdb(access_key,secret_key)
>>>
```

Creating a domain with Python

A SimpleDB domain is a container for storing data, and is similar in concept to a table in a relational database. A new domain can be created by specifying a name for the domain.

```
>>> domain1 = sdb_connection.create_domain('prabhakar-dom-1')
>>>
```

Retrieving a domain with Python

Retrieving a list of all our domains will return a Python result set object that can be iterated over in order to access each domain.

```
>>> all_domains = sdb_connection.get_all_domains()
>>>
>>> len(all_domains)
1
>>>
>>> for d in all_domains:
...     print d.name
...
prabhakar-dom-1
```

You can also retrieve a single domain by specifying its name.

```
>>> my_domain = sdb_connection.get_domain('prabhakar-dom-1')
>>>
>>> print my_domain.name
prabhakar-dom-1
```

Creating items with Python

You can create a new item by specifying the attributes for the item along with the name of the item to be created.

```
>>>
>>> my_domain.put_attributes('car1', {'make':'BMW', 'color':'grey','year'
:'2008','desc':'Sedan','model':'530i'})
>>>
```

```
>>> my_domain.put_attributes('car2', {'make':'BMW', 'color':'white','year
':'2007','desc':' Sports Utility Vehicle','model':'X5'})

>>>
```

Items stored within a domain can be retrieved by specifying the item name. The name of an item must be unique and is similar to the concept of a primary key in a relational database. The uniqueness of the item name within a domain will cause your existing item attributes to be overwritten with the new values if you try to store new attributes with the same item name.

```
>>> my_item = my_domain.get_item('car1')

>>>

>>> print my_item
{u'color': u'grey', u'model': u'530i', u'desc': u'Sedan', u'make':
u'BMW', u'year': u'2008'}

>>>
```

You can query for items within a domain by specifying the attribute and value to match. The SELECT syntax is a new addition to SimpleDB and allows searching your domains using simple SQL-like query expressions. The previous version of SimpleDB only supported a query-style syntax that is now being deprecated in favor of the simpler and easier-to-use SELECT expressions.

```
>>> rs = my_domain.select("SELECT name FROM `prabhakar-dom-1`
    WHERE make='BMW'")
>>> for result in rs:
...     print result.name
...
car1
car2
>>>
```

Multiple attributes can also be specified as a part of the query.

```
>>> rs = my_domain.select("SELECT name FROM `prabhakar-dom-1`
                    WHERE make='BMW' AND model='X5'")
>>> for result in rs:
...     print result.name
...
car2
>>>
```

You can delete a specific item and all of its attributes from a domain.

```
>>> sdb_connection.get_attributes('prabhakar-dom-1','car1')
{u'color': u'grey', u'model': u'530i', u'desc': u'Sedan',
    u'make': u'BMW', u'year': u'2008'}
>>>
>>> sdb_connection.delete_attributes('prabhakar-dom-1','car1')
True
>>> sdb_connection.get_attributes('prabhakar-dom-1',car1')
{}
>>>
```

Finally, you delete a domain by specifying its name. Once you delete a domain, the data is gone forever. So use caution when deleting a domain!

```
>>> sdb_connection.delete_domain('prabhakar-dom-1')
True
>>>
```

Summary

In this chapter, we set up an AWS account, enabled SimpleDB service for the account, and installed and set up libraries for Java, PHP, and Python. We explored several SimpleDB operations using these libraries. In the next chapter, we will examine the differences between SimpleDB and the relational database model in detail.

3
SimpleDB versus RDBMS

We have all used a **Relational Database Management System (RDBMS)** at some point in our careers. These relational databases are ubiquitous and are available from a wide range of companies such as Oracle, Microsoft, IBM, and so on. These databases have served us well for our application needs. However, there is a new breed of applications coming to the forefront in the current Internet-driven and socially networked economy. The new applications require large scaling to meet demand peaks that can quickly reach massive levels. This is a scenario that is hard to satisfy using a traditional relational database, as it is impossible to requisition and provision the hardware and software resources that will be needed to service the demand peaks. It is also non-trivial and difficult to scale a normal RDBMS to hundreds or thousands of nodes. The overwhelming complexity of doing this makes the RDBMS not viable for these kinds of applications. SimpleDB provides a great alternative to an RDBMS and can provide a solution to all these problems. However, in order to provide this solution, SimpleDB makes some choices and design decisions that you need to understand in order to make an informed choice about the data storage for your application domain.

In this chapter, we are going to discuss the differences between SimpleDB and a traditional RDBMS, as well as the pros and cons of using SimpleDB as the storage engine in your application.

No normalization

Normalization is a process of organizing data efficiently in a relational database by eliminating redundant data, while at the same time ensuring that the data dependencies make sense. SimpleDB data models do not conform to any of the normalization forms, and tend to be completely de-normalized. The lack of need for normalization in SimpleDB allows you a great deal of flexibility with your model, and enables you to use the power of multi-valued attributes in your data.

Let's look at a simple example of a database starting with a basic spreadsheet structure and then design it for an RDBMS and a SimpleDB. In this example, we will create a simple contact database, with contact information as raw data.

ID	First_Name	Last_Name	Phone_Num
101	John	Smith	555-845-7854
101	John	Smith	555-854-9885
101	John	Smith	555-695-7485
102	Bill	Jones	555-748-7854
102	Bill	Jones	555-874-8654

The obvious issue is the repetition of the name data. The table is inefficient and would require care to update to keep the name data in sync. To find a person by his or her phone number is easy.

```
SELECT * FROM Contact_Info WHERE Phone_Num = '555-854-9885'
```

So let's analyze the strengths and weaknesses of this database design.

SCORE—Raw data	Strength	Weakness
Efficient storage		No
Efficient search by phone number	Yes	
Efficient search by name		No
Easy to add another phone number	Yes	

The design is simple, but as the name data is repeated, it would require care to keep the data in sync. Searching for phone numbers by name would be ugly if the names got out of sync.

To improve the design, we can rationalize the data. One approach would be to create multiple phone number fields such as the following. While this is a simple solution, it does limit the phone numbers to three. Add e-mail and Twitter, and the table becomes wider and wider.

ID	First_Name	Last_Name	Phone_Num_1	Phone_Num_2	Phone_Num_3
101	John	Smith	555-845-7854	555-854-9885	555-695-7485
102	Bill	Jones	555-748-7854	555-874-8654	

Finding a person by a phone number is ugly.

```
SELECT * FROM Contact_Info WHERE Phone_Num_1 = '555-854-9885'
OR Phone_Num_2 = '555-854-9885'
OR Phone_Num_3 = '555-854-9885'
```

Now let's analyze the strengths and weaknesses of this database design.

SCORE—Rationalize data	Strength	Weakness
Efficient storage	Yes	
Efficient search by phone number		No
Efficient search by name	Yes	
Easy to add another phone number		No

The design is simple, but the phone numbers are limited to three, and searching by phone number involves three index searches.

Another approach would be to use a delimited list for the phone number as follows:

ID	First_Name	Last_Name	Phone_Nums
101	John	Smith	555-845-7854;555-854-9885;555-695-7485
102	Bill	Jones	555-748-7854;555-874-8654

This approach has the advantage of no data repetition and is easy to maintain, compact, and extendable, but the only way to find a record by the phone number is with a substring search.

```
SELECT * FROM Contact_Info WHERE Phone_Nums LIKE %555-854-9885%
```

This type of SQL forces a complete table scan. Do this with a small table and no one will notice, but try this on a large database with millions of records, and the performance of the database will suffer.

SCORE—Delimited data	Strength	Weakness
Efficient storage	Yes	
Efficient search by phone number		No
Efficient search by name	Yes	
Easy to add another phone number	Yes	

A delimited field is good for data that is of one type and will only be retrieved.

The **normalization** for relational databases results in splitting up your data into separate tables that are related to one another by keys. A **join** is an operation that allows you to retrieve the data back easily across the multiple tables.

Let's first normalize this data.

This is the `Person_Info` table:

ID	First_Name	Last_Name
101	John	Smith
102	Bill	Jones

And this is the `Phone_Info` table:

ID	Phone_Num
101	555-845-7854
101	555-854-9885
101	555-695-7485
102	555-748-7854
102	555-874-8654

Now a join of the `Person_Info` table with the `Phone_Info` can retrieve the list of phone numbers as well as the e-mail addresses. The table structure is clean and other than the ID primary key, no data is duplicated. Provided `Phone_Num` is indexed, retrieving a contact by the phone number is efficient.

```
SELECT First_Name, Last_Name, Phone_num, Person_Info.ID
FROM Person_Info JOIN Phone_Info
ON Person_Info.ID = Phone_Info.ID
WHERE Phone_Num = '555-854-9885'
```

So if we analyze the strengths and weaknesses of this database design, we get:

SCORE – Relational data	Strength	Weakness
Efficient storage	Yes	
Efficient search by phone number	Yes	
Efficient search by name	Yes	
Easy to add another phone number	Yes	

While this is an efficient relational model, there is no `join` command in SimpleDB. Using two tables would force two selects to retrieve the complete contact information. Let's look at how this would be done using the SimpleDB principles.

No joins

SimpleDB does not support the concept of joins. Instead, SimpleDB provides you with the ability to store multiple values for an attribute, thus avoiding the necessity to perform a join to retrieve all the values.

ID			
101	First_Name=John	Last_Name=Smith	Phone_Num = 555-845-7854 Phone_Num = 555-854-9885 Phone_Num = 555-695-7485
102	First_Name=Bill	Last_Name=Jones	Phone_Num = 555-748-7854 Phone_Num = 555-874-8654

In the SimpleDB table, each record is stored as an item with attribute/value pairs. The difference here is that the `Phone_Num` field has multiple values. Unlike a delimited list field, SimpleDB indexes all values enabling an efficient search each value.

```
SELECT * FROM Contact_Info WHERE Phone_Num = '555-854-9885'
```

This `SELECT` is very quick and efficient. It is even possible to use `Phone_Num` multiple times such as follows:

```
SELECT * FROM Contact_Info WHERE Phone_Num = '555-854-9885'
OR Phone_Num = '555-748-7854'
```

Let's analyze the strengths and weaknesses of this approach:

SCORE—SimpleDB data	Strength	Weakness
Efficient storage	Yes	
Efficient search by phone number	Yes	
Efficient search by name	Yes	
Easy to add another phone number	Yes	

No schemas

There are no schemas anywhere in sight of SimpleDB. You don't have to create schemas, change schemas, migrate schemas to a new version, or maintain schemas. This is yet another thing that is difficult for some people from a traditional relational database world to grasp, but this flexibility is one of the keys to the power of scaling offered by SimpleDB. You can store any attribute-value data you like in any way you want. If the requirements for your application should suddenly change and you need to start storing data on a customer's Twitter handle for instance, all you need to do is store the data without worrying about any schema changes!

Let's add an e-mail address to the database in the previous example. In the relational database, it is necessary to either add e-mail to the phone table with a type of contact field or add another field. Let's add another table named Email_Info.

Person_Info table:

ID	First_Name	Last_Name
101	John	Smith
102	Bill	Jones

Phone_Info table:

ID	Phone_Num
101	555-845-7854
101	555-854-9885
101	555-695-7485
102	555-748-7854
102	555-874-8654

Email_Info table:

ID	Email_Addr
101	john@abc.ccc
102	bill@def.ccc

Using a traditional relational database approach, we join the three tables to extract the requested data in one call.

```
SELECT First_Name, Last_Name, Phone_num, Person_Info.ID, Email_Addr
FROM Person_Info JOIN Phone_Info JOIN Email_Info
ON Person_Info.ID = Phone_Info.ID
AND Person_Info.ID = Email_Info.ID
WHERE Phone_Num = '555-854-9885'
```

Now let's analyze the strengths and weaknesses of this approach:

SCORE — Relational data	Strength	Weakness
Efficient storage	Yes	
Efficient search by phone number, email	Yes	
Efficient search by name	Yes	
Easy to add another phone number	Yes	
Expandable	Yes	New table defined Two joins required

We ignored the issue of join versus **left outer join**, which is really what should be used here unless all contacts have a phone number and e-mail address. The example is just to illustrate that the `Contact_Info` schema must be modified.

`Contact_Info` domain:

ID			
101	First_Name = John	Last_Name = Smith	Phone_Num = 555-845-7854 Phone_Num = 555-854-9885 Phone_Num = 555-695-7485
			Email_Addr = john@abc.ccc
102	First_Name = Bill	Last_Name = Jones	Phone_Num = 555-748-7854 Phone_Num = 555-874-8654
			Email_Addr = john@def.ccc

The obvious question is why is `Email_Addr` not in its own column? In SimpleDB, there is no concept of a column in a table. The spreadsheet view of the SimpleDB data was done for ease of readability, not because it reflects the data structure. The only structure in SimpleDB consists of the item name and attribute/value pairs. The proper representation of the SimpleDB data is:

ID	Attribute/Value pairs
101	First_Name = John Last_Name = Smith Phone_Num = 555-845-7854 Phone_Num = 555-854-9885 Phone_Num = 555-695-7485 Email_Addr = john@abc.ccc
102	First_Name = Bill Last_Name = Jones Phone_Num = 555-748-7854 Phone_Num = 555-874-8654 Email_Addr = john@def.ccc

Use the following query to fetch a contact item by the e-mail address:

```
SELECT * FROM Contact_Info WHERE Email_Addr = 'john@def.ccc'
```

Let's analyze the strengths and weaknesses of this approach:

SCORE – SimpleDB data	Strength	Weakness
Efficient storage	Yes	
Efficient search by phone number, email	Yes	
Efficient search by name	Yes	
Easy to add another phone number	Yes	
Expandable	Yes	

Simpler SQL

Structured Query Language (**SQL**) is a standard language that is widely used for accessing and manipulating the data stored in a relational database. SQL has evolved over the years into a highly complex language that can do a vast variety of things to your database. SimpleDB does not support the complete SQL language, but instead it lets you perform your data retrieval using a much smaller and simpler subset of an SQL-like query language. This simplifies the whole process of querying your data. A big difference between the simpler SQL supported by SimpleDB and SQL is the support for multi-valued SimpleDB attributes, which makes it super simple to query your data and get back multiple values for an attribute.

The syntax of the SimpleDB SQL is summarized in this syntax:

```
select output_list
from domain_name
[where expression]
[sort_instructions]
[limit limit]
```

Only strings

SimpleDB uses a very simple data model, and all data is stored as an UTF-8 string. This simplified textual data makes it easy for SimpleDB to automatically index your data and give you the ability to retrieve the data very quickly. If you need to store and retrieve other kinds of data types such as numbers and dates, you must encode these data types into strings whose lexicographical ordering will be the same as your intended ordering of the data. As SimpleDB does not have the concept of schemas that enforce type correctness for your domains, it is the developer's responsibility to ensure the correct encoding of data before storage into SimpleDB.

Working only in strings impacts two aspects of using the database: queries and sorts.

Consider the following `Sample_Qty` table:

ID	
101	Quantity = 1.0
102	Quantity = 1.00
103	Quantity = 10
104	Quantity = 25
105	Quantity = 100

Now try and execute the following SQL statement:

```
SELECT * FROM Sample_Qty WHERE Quantity= '1'
```

This SQL statement will retrieve nothing—not even items 101 and 102.

Selecting all records sorted by Quantity will return the order 101, 102, 103, 105, 104.

Dates present an easier problem, as they can be stored in ISO 8601 format to enable sorting as well as predictable searching.

Eventual consistency

Simple DB can be thought of as a Write-Seldom-Read-Many model. Updates are done to a central database, but reads can be done from many read-only database slave servers.

SimpleDB keeps multiple copies of each domain. Whenever data is written or updated within a domain, first a success status code is returned to your application, and then all the different copies of the data are updated. The propagation of these changes to all of the nodes at all the storage locations might take some time, but eventually the data will become consistent across all the nodes.

SimpleDB provides this assurance only of eventual consistency for your data. This means that the data you retrieve from SimpleDB at any particular time may be slightly out of date. The main reason for this is that SimpleDB service is implemented as a distributed system, and all of the information is stored across multiple physical servers and potentially across multiple data centers in a completely redundant manner. This ensures the large-scale ready accessibility and safety of your data, but comes at the cost of a slight delay before any addition, alteration, or deletion operations you perform on the data being propagated throughout the entire distributed SimpleDB system. Your data will eventually be globally consistent, but until it is consistent, the possibility of retrieving slightly outdated information from SimpleDB exists.

Amazon has stated in the past that states of global consistency across all the nodes will usually be achieved "within seconds"; however, please be aware that this timeframe will depend to a great degree on the processing and the network load on SimpleDB at the time that you make a change to your data. An intermediate caching layer can quickly solve this consistency issue if data consistency is highly important and essential to your application. The principle of eventual consistency is the hardest to grasp, and it is the biggest difference between a RDBMS and SimpleDB. In order to scale massively, this is a trade-off that needs to be made at design time for your application. If you consider how often you will require immediate consistency within your web applications, you might find that this trade-off is well worth the improved scalability of your application.

Flash: February 24, 2010 — consistent read added

While eventual consistency is still the normal mode for SimpleDB, Amazon announced several extensions for consistent read. When using a `GetAttributes` or `SELECT`, the `ConsistentRead = true` can be selected, forcing a read of the most current value. This tells SimpleDB to read the items from the master database rather than from one of the slaves, guaranteeing the latest updates or deletes. This does not mean you can use this on all reads and still get the extreme scaling.

A conditional PUT or DELETE was also announced, which will execute a database PUT or DELETE only if the consistent read of a specific attribute has a specific value or does not exist. This is useful if concurrent controls or counters primitives.

Scalability

Relational databases are designed around the entities and the relationships between the entities, and need a large investment in hardware and servers in order to provide high scaling. SimpleDB provides a great alternative that is designed around partitioning your data into independent chunks that are stored in a distributed manner and can scale up massively. SimpleDB provides the automatic partitioning and replication of your data, while at the same time guaranteeing fast access and reliability for your data. You can let Amazon scale their platform as needed using their extensive resources, while you enjoy the ability to easily scale up in response to increased demand!

The best feature of SimpleDB scalability is that you only pay for usage, not for the large cluster needed in anticipation of large usage.

Low maintenance

Maintaining a relational database and keeping it humming with indexing takes effort, know-how, and technical and administrative resources. Applications are not static but dynamic things, and change constantly along with additions of new features. All of these updates can result in changes and modifications to the database schema along with increased maintenance and tuning costs. SimpleDB is hosted and maintained for you by Amazon. Your task is as simple as storing your data and retrieving it when needed. The simplicity of structured data and lack of schemas helps your application be more flexible and adaptable to change, which is always around the corner. SimpleDB ensures that your queries are optimized and retrieval times are fast by indexing all your data automatically.

Advantages of the SimpleDB model

SimpleDB's alternative approach for storing data can be advantageous for meeting your application needs when compared to a traditional relational database. Here's the list of advantages:

- Reduced maintenance as compared to a relational database
- Automated indexing of your data for fast performance
- Flexibility to modify or change your stored data without the need to worry about schemas
- Failover for your data automatically being provided by Amazon
- Replication for your data across multiple nodes also handled for you by Amazon
- Ability to easily scale up in response to increased demand without worrying about running out of hardware or processing capacity
- Simplified data storage and querying using a simple API
- The lack of object-to-relational mapping that is common for an RDBMS allows your structured data to map more directly to your underlying application code and reduce the application development time

Disadvantages of the SimpleDB model

SimpleDB's alternative approach also has some disadvantages compared to a relational database for certain applications.

- Those using applications that always need to ensure immediate consistency of data will find that SimpleDB's eventual data consistency model may not suit their needs. The consistent read announcement does change this, but the eventual consistency model is still the basis of the extreme scalability.

- Using SimpleDB as the data storage engine in your applications needs the development team to get used to different concepts over a simple, traditional RDBMS.

- Because relationships are not explicitly defined at the schema level as in a relational database, you might need to enforce some data constraints within your application code.

- If your application needs to store data other than strings, such as numbers and dates, additional effort will be required on your part to encode the strings before storing them in the SimpleDB format.

- The ability to have multiple attributes for an item is a completely different way of storing data and has a learning curve attached to it for new users who are exposed to SimpleDB.

Summary

In this chapter, we discussed the differences between SimpleDB and the traditional relational database systems in detail. In the next chapter, we are going to review the data model used by SimpleDB.

4

The SimpleDB Data Model

The entire data model for SimpleDB is comprised of four concepts—domains, items, attributes, and values. We will explore these concepts in detail in this chapter. The conceptual hierarchy of a domain in SimpleDB is like the following chart and shows the relation between the different components.

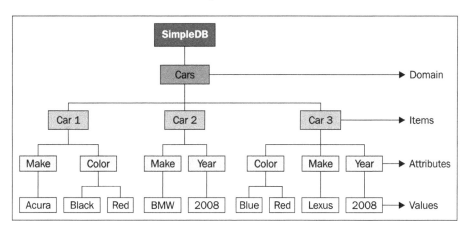

In this chapter, we will cover:

- Interacting with a domain
- Metadata for a domain
- Interacting with items in a domain
- Interacting with the attributes of an item
- Storing multiple values for an attribute
- SimpleDB constraints on domain, items, attributes, and attribute values
- Consistent Read and Conditional Put/Delete announced on February 24, 2010

Domains

A **domain** is a container that lets you store your structured data and run queries against it. The data is stored in the domain as **items**. A domain is similar to a worksheet tab in a spreadsheet, while items are similar in concept to the rows in the spreadsheet. You can run queries against a domain, but you cannot yet query across domains in the current version of SimpleDB. Each domain in your SimpleDB account is completely distinct from all your other domains, and therefore the items stored in one domain are completely separate from the items stored in other domains. This is why queries cannot be performed across domains. You can place all of your data in a single domain or partition it across multiple domains, depending on the nature of the data and the application. You can create a domain called *cars* and use it or you can partition the data into separate domains such as brands beginning with A-J in CARSAJ, beginning with K-T in CARSKT, and so on. SimpleDB gives you the freedom to partition the data however you like.

Domains with Java

You can create a domain using the `SimpleDB` class in Typica.

```
SimpleDB sdb = new SimpleDB(awsAccessId, awsSecretKey, true);
try {
    Domain domain = sdb.createDomain("Cars");
    System.out.println(domain.getName());
} catch (SDBException ex) {
    System.out.println(ex.getMessage());
}
```

Typica provides several methods for interacting with a domain and performing various operations on it.

- `batchPutAttributes`: This method is used to batch-insert multiple items without attributes.

- `deleteItem`: This method is used to delete an item.

- `getItem`: This method is used to get an item object without getting a list of them.

- `getItemsAttributes`: This method is used to get attributes of given items.

- `getMetadata`: This method is used to returns information about the domain.

- `getName`: This method is used to get the name of the domain represented by this object.

- `listItems`: This method is used to get a list of all items in this domain.

- `listItemsAttributes`: This method is used to get attributes of items specified in the query string.

- `listItemsWithAttributes`: This method is used to get a list of items (with attributes) in this domain filtered by the query string.

Domains with PHP

You can create a domain in PHP with the following:

```
$sdb = new SimpleDB(awsAccessKey, awsSecretKey);
$sdb->createDomain("Cars");
```

Our sample PHP library provides a number of functions for accessing SimpleDB:

- `deleteDomain`: This method is used to delete a domain.

- `listDomains`: This method is used to list all domains.

- `domainMetadata`: This method is used to return information about a specific domain.

- `select`: This method is used to get the attributes/values for an SQL query.

- `getAttributes`: This method is used to get the attributes/values for a specific item.

- `putAttributes`: This method is used to put the attributes/values for a specific item.

- `batchPutAttributes`: This method is used to batch-put attributes/values for a group of items.

- `deleteAttributes`: This method is used to delete attributes/values for a specific item.

 The SDB-PHP API supports the newly-added capabilities of Consistent Read and Conditional Put/Delete from February 24, 2010.

Domains with Python

Here is how you would create the same `Cars` domain using **boto**:

```
>>>cars__domain = sdb_connection.create_domain('Cars')
Domain:Cars
>>>
```

The domain object created here provides all of the methods that we need for interacting with the Cars domain.

You can use the inspect module to list all of the boto methods for interacting with a domain.

```
>>>importinspect
>>>
>>> import pprint
>>> pp = pprint.PrettyPrinter(indent=4)
>>>
>>> pp.pprint(inspect.getmembers(cars_domain, inspect.ismethod))
[   ('__init__', <bound method Domain.__init__ of Domain:Cars>),
    ('__iter__', <bound method Domain.__iter__ of Domain:Cars>),
    ('__repr__', <bound method Domain.__repr__ of Domain:Cars>),
    (   'batch_put_attributes',
<bound method Domain.batch_put_attributes of Domain:Cars>),
    (   'delete_attributes',
<bound method Domain.delete_attributes of Domain:Cars>),
    ('delete_item', <bound method Domain.delete_item of Domain:Cars>),
    ('endElement', <bound method Domain.endElement of Domain:Cars>),
    ('from_xml', <bound method Domain.from_xml of Domain:Cars>),
    ('get_attributes', <bound method Domain.get_attributes of
Domain:Cars>),
    ('get_item', <bound method Domain.get_item of Domain:Cars>),
     ('get_metadata', <bound method Domain.get_metadata of Domain:Cars>),
    ('new_item', <bound method Domain.new_item of Domain:Cars>),
    ('put_attributes', <bound method Domain.put_attributes of
Domain:Cars>),
    ('query', <bound method Domain.query of Domain:Cars>),
    ('select', <bound method Domain.select of Domain:Cars>),
    ('startElement', <bound method Domain.startElement of Domain:Cars>),
    ('to_xml', <bound method Domain.to_xml of Domain:Cars>)]
>>>
```

The methods provided by **boto** for interacting with a domain are as follows:

- `batch_put_attributes`: This method is used to store attributes for multiple items with a single call. This is a nice way to batch things together to avoid the overhead of making multiple calls to SimpleDB, each of which stores attributes for a single item.

- `delete_attributes`: This method is used to delete the attributes from a given item.

- `delete_item`: This method is used to delete the specified item from the domain.

- `get_attributes`: This method is used to retrieve the attributes for a given item. You can either get all the attributes for an item, or specify the names of attributes of interest.

- `get_item`: This method is used to retrieve the specified item and all its attributes from the domain.

- `put_attributes`: This method is used to store attributes for a given item.

- `query`: This method is used to return a list of items within domain that match the query.

- `select`: This method is used to return a set of attributes for item names within the domain that match the query expression. The query must be expressed in using the recently-introduced SELECT-style syntax rather than the original SimpleDB query language.

Exploring the metadata for a domain and costs

Every call made to SimpleDB, irrespective of whether the operation works on a domain or an item, always returns two specific values associated with it. These values are automatically provided within the response. They exist for all operations, and for every invocation of the operation in SimpleDB:

- `RequestId`: A unique ID for tracking the request made to SimpleDB. This is also very useful for debugging purposes. If you are having any issues with your calls to SimpleDB and are unable to determine the cause or reason from your side, this is the ID that you need to give AWS as a part of the debug information to facilitate tracing the request.

- `BoxUsage`: SimpleDB measures the machine utilization of each request and charges the customer based on the amount of machine capacity used to complete the particular request (SELECT, GET, PUT, and so on), normalized to the hourly capacity of a circa 2007 1.7 GHz Xeon processor. This measure is named as **BoxUsage** and its value is returned as part of the response for every call made to SimpleDB. BoxUsage is a number that you can use for tuning your queries based on the fact that the longer a query takes to run, the higher its BoxUsage value.

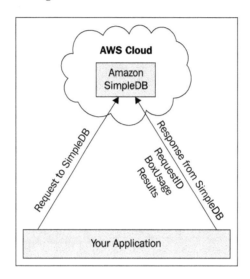

Colin Percival has a great dissection of the BoxUsage values returned by SimpleDB on his blog (`http://www.daemonology.net/blog/2008-06-25-dissecting-simpledb-boxusage.html`) and provides this breakdown of the costs associated with the calls made to SimpleDB.

Request type	BoxUsage (hours)	BoxUsage (seconds)	Overhead cost (μ$)	Variable cost (μ$)
CreateDomain DeleteDomain	0.0055590278	4803 / 240	778.264	
ListDomains	0.0000071759	(6 + 1/5) / 240	1.005	
PutAttributes (N attributes specified) DeleteAttributes (N attributes specified)	0.0000219907 + 0.0000000002 N^3	19 / 240 + 0.00000072 N^3	3.079	0.000028 N^3
GetAttributes (N values returned)	0.0000093202 + 0.0000000020 N^2	(8 + 1/19) / 240 + 0.00000720 N^2	1.305	0.000280 N^2

Request type	BoxUsage (hours)	BoxUsage (seconds)	Overhead cost (μ$)	Variable cost (μ$)
Query (N items returned)	0.0000140000 + 0.0000000080 N or more	0.0504 + 0.00002880 N or more	1.960	0.001120 N or more

 These numbers and the associated costs for each type of SimpleDB are interesting, but please keep in mind that these costs will change as AWS adjusts the service and changes the pricing.

The costs incurred by you when using SimpleDB also include the cost for storing the actual data, which is separate from the BoxUsage values.

Retrieving domain metadata

You can also retrieve system statistics about the data contained within a specified domain. These statistics provide some very useful metadata that can give you a good idea about how you are using SimpleDB.

Retrieving domain metadata with Java

Typica provides a method named `getMetadata()` on a domain object that can be used for retrieving the metadata information. You can retrieve the values for the `requestID` and `boxusage` for every call that is made to SimpleDB.

```
SimpleDB sdb = new SimpleDB(awsAccessId, awsSecretKey, true);
try {
    Domain domain = sdb.getDomain("songs");
    DomainMetadataResult metadata = domain.getMetadata();
    System.out.println(" ItemCount: " + metadata.getItemCount());
    System.out.println(" AttributeNameCount: "
                    + metadata.getAttributeNameCount());
    System.out.println(" AttributeValueCount: "
                    + metadata.getAttributeValueCount());
    System.out.println(" ItemNamesSizeBytes: "
                    + metadata.getItemNamesSizeBytes());
    System.out.println(" AttributeNamesSizeBytes: "
                    + metadata.getAttributeNamesSizeBytes());
    System.out.println(" AttributeValuesSizeBytes: "
                    + metadata.getAttributeValuesSizeBytes());
    System.out.println(" Timestamp: " + metadata.getTimestamp());
```

```
        System.out.println(" BoxUsage: " + metadata.getBoxUsage());
        System.out.println(" RequestID: " + metadata.getRequestId());
    } catch (SDBException ex) {
        System.out.println(ex.getMessage());
    }
```

Retrieving domain metadata with PHP

The domainMetadata function returns an array of values for an existing domain. If the domain does not exist; an error is returned.

```
$sdb = new SimpleDB(awsAccessKey, awsSecretKey);
    // create connection
$domain = "car-s";
$rest = $sdb->domainMetadata($domainName);
    // returns an array with names
echo("ItemCount: ".$rest["ItemCount"]."\n");
echo("ItemNamesSizeBytes: ".$rest["ItemNamesSizeBytes"]."\n");
echo("AttributeNameCount: ".$rest["AttributeNameCount"]."\n");
echo("AttributeNamesSizeBytes: "
    .$rest["AttributeNamesSizeBytes"]."\n");
echo("AttributeValueCount: ".$rest["AttributeValueCount"]."\n");
echo("AttributeValuesSizeBytes: "
    .$rest["AttributeValuesSizeBytes"]."\n");
echo("Timestamp: ".$rest["Timestamp"]." "
    . date("M j,Y g:iA",$rest["Timestamp"]) . "\n");
echo("RequestId: ".$sdb->RequestId."\n");
echo("BoxUsage: ".$sdb->BoxUsage." = "
    . SimpleDB::displayUsage($sdb->BoxUsage)."<br>");
```

Accessing the values is a simple array reference. Using the domain metadata call is a low-cost way to validate that a specific domain exists.

Retrieving domain metadata with Python

Boto provides the box usage and request ID values for each call that we make to SimpleDB, as attributes on the object that is returned as a result of the call. In case of the domain that we created above, for instance, we can easily get these values from the cars_domain object.

```
>>>
>>> cars_domain.BoxUsage
u'0.0000091640'
>>>
>>> cars_domain.RequestId
```

```
u'6d7a96bd-6ac5-828c-9a48-ec5fa1920803'
>>>
>>>
>>>
>>> cars_metadata = cars_domain.get_metadata()
>>>
>>> cars_metadata.attr_name_count
0
>>>
>>> cars_metadata.attr_names_size
0
>>>
>>> cars_metadata.attr_value_count
0
>>>
>>> cars_metadata.attr_values_size
0
>>>
>>> cars_metadata.item_count
0
>>>
>>> cars_metadata.item_names_size
0
>>>
>>> cars_metadata.timestamp
u'1254073990'
>>>
>>> cars_metadata.BoxUsage
u'0.0000071759'
>>>
>>> cars_metadata.RequestId
u'65fa544a-036b-b897-2fd7-cb50a4b5cfc2'
>>>
```

Components of a domain's metadata

The metadata associated with each domain is:

- Date and time the metadata was last updated.

- Number of all items in the domain. The SELECT API now includes a `count` keyword that can be used for getting much more useful item counts than this specific metadata.

- Number of all attribute's name/value pairs in the domain.

- Number of unique attribute names in the domain.

- Total size of all item names in the domain, in bytes.

- Total size of all attribute values, in bytes.

- Total size of all unique attribute names, in bytes.

The following figure displays visually the various components that comprise the metadata for a SimpleDB domain:

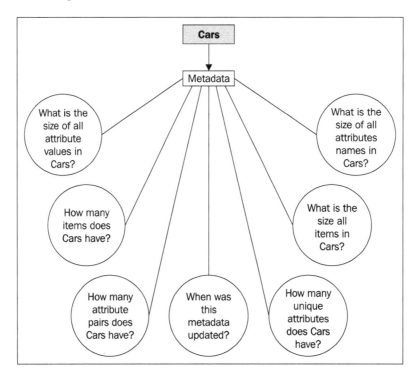

SimpleDB domain constraints

You should also be familiar with some of the constraints and limitations when using the SimpleDB domains.

- **Number of domains**: Each SimpleDB account is by default allowed to create up to 100 domains. If your architecture or system design should need more than 100 domains, you can request AWS to increase the limit. Normally it takes about two business days for the request to be approved. You need to fill out a form on the SimpleDB site (http://aws.amazon.com/contact-us/simpledb-limit-request/) to submit your request.

- **Size of domain**: The size of a single domain is limited to 10 GB of data. This includes all the storage used by the data for the domain. This is a hard limit and currently there is no way to request for an increase.

- **Number of attributes**: The total number of attributes stored in a domain is limited to one billion per domain. That is a lot of attributes, and most applications should comfortably fit within this limit. This is considered per domain, so with the default number of 100 domains, you are looking at a total allowed limit of 100 billion attributes! Partitioning data across multiple domains can be used to get around the limit.

- **Name of a domain**: The name of a domain must be at least three characters in length and a maximum of 255 characters. The allowed characters in the name are a-z, A-Z, 0-9, _, ., and -.

Items

Items represent individual objects within each domain, and each item contains attributes with values. Each item is conceptually similar to a row in a spreadsheet. Items are distinguished by the presence of a unique ID, which can also be used when querying for a specific item.

 This unique identifier is not automatically provided by SimpleDB, and is the responsibility of the developer.

A common scheme followed by users of SimpleDB is to generate **Globally Unique Identifiers** or **GUIDs** and use them as the key for each item. You are not required to use this scheme and are free to generate this ID anyway you like as long as it is unique. The ID also needs to be unique only within the domain of interest.

The February 24, 2010 announcement added capabilities that aid in doing a counter GUID. The Consistent Read and Conditional Put/Delete capabilities are documented at the end of this chapter.

You can add attributes to an item in SimpleDB. Any items that you create that do not have any attributes will not be returned in queries.

 SimpleDB treats empty items as non-existent.

Adding attributes to an item with Java

You must create a list of attributes and then add those attributes to an item in your domain when using Typica.

```java
SimpleDB sdb = new SimpleDB(awsAccessId, awsSecretKey, true);
try {
    Domain domain = sdb.getDomain("Cars");
    Item item = domain.getItem("Car 1");
    List<ItemAttribute> list = new ArrayList<ItemAttribute>();
    list.add(new ItemAttribute("make", "BMW", false));
    list.add(new ItemAttribute("color", "Black", false));
    item.putAttributes(list);

    Item saved_item = domain.getItem("Car 1");
    for (ItemAttribute attr : saved_item.getAttributes()) {
        System.out.println("  " + attr.getName() + " = " + attr
            .getValue());
    }
    item = domain.getItem("Car 1");
    list = new ArrayList<ItemAttribute>();
    list.add(new ItemAttribute("make", "BMW", true));
    list.add(new ItemAttribute("color", "Blue", true));
    item.putAttributes(list);

    Item updated_item = domain.getItem("Car 1");
    for (ItemAttribute attr : updated_item.getAttributes()) {
        System.out.println("  " + attr.getName() + " = " + attr
            .getValue());
    }
    domain.deleteItem("Car 1");
} catch (SDBException ex) {
    System.out.println(ex.getMessage());
}
```

Adding attributes to an item with PHP

You can use the `putAttributes` method on an SDB connection object to add
an item, and specify the domain, a unique name for the item, and the list of
attributes for the item.

```php
$sdb = new SimpleDB(awsAccessKey, awsSecretKey);
  // create connection

$domain = "car-s";

$item_name = "car1";
echo "putAttributes() record 1<br>";
$putAttributesRequest["make"] = array("value" => "Acura");
  // Example add an attribute
$putAttributesRequest["color"] =
    array("value" => array("Black","Red"));
  // Add multiple values

$rest = $sdb->
    putAttributes($domain,$item_name,$putAttributesRequest);
if ($rest) {
    echo("Record $item_name created");
    echo("RequestId: ".$sdb->RequestId."<br>");
    echo("BoxUsage: ".$sdb->BoxUsage." = "
        . SimpleDB::displayUsage($sdb->BoxUsage)."<br>");
} else {
    echo("Record $item_name FAILED<br>");
    echo("ErrorCode: ".$sdb->ErrorCode."<p>");
}
```

In this example, item `car1` is put into domain `car-s`. Two attributes are added to
item `car1`: attribute `make` with value `Acura` and attribute `color` with two values
`Black` and `Red`.

Adding attributes to an item with Python

You can use the `put_attributes` method on an SDB connection object to add an
item, and specify the domain, a unique name for the item, and the list of attributes
for the item.

```python
>>>
>>> item1 = sdb_connection.put_attributes('Cars','Car 1', {})
>>> cars_domain.get_item('Car 1')
>>>
```

You can also use the `put_attributes()` method that is available on a domain object to add a new item in exactly the same way.

```
>>> item2 = cars_domain.put_attributes('Car 2',{'make':'BMW',
'color':'Black'})

>>>

>>> cars_domain.get_item('Car 2')

{u'color': u'Black', u'make': u'BMW'}

>>>
```

The query for the item `Car 2` returned the item as the item was not empty and already had attributes. Now we will add attributes to the empty item and then watch it show up again when we try to get the item from the domain! You can replace the attributes for an item by specifying a true value for the replace parameter in the `put_attributes()` method.

```
>>> item1 = cars_domain.put_attributes('Car 1',{'make':'BMW',
'color':'Black'},True)

>>> cars_domain.get_item('Car 1')

{u'color': u'Black', u'make': u'BMW'}

>>>
```

The methods and fields provided by **boto** on an item object for interacting with the item are:

- `add_value`: This method will add a new attribute key and value to the item. It makes sure you call `save()` to actually persist your additions to SimpleDB.

- `get`: This method will retrieve the value of the specified attribute for the item.

- `delete`: This method will delete all the attributes for the item.

- `has_key`: This method will check if the item has the specified attribute.

- `iterkeys`: This method will retrieve an iterator that will let you iterate through the attributes keys for the item.

- `itervalues`: This method will retrieve an iterator that will let you iterate through the attributes values for the item.

- `keys`: This method will return a list of all the attribute keys for the item.

- `values`: This method will return a list of all the attribute values for the item.

- `load`: This method will reload the item's state from SimpleDB. Be careful when using this method. If you make changes to your item locally, but do not persist those changes to SimpleDB by calling `save()`, then this method will overwrite those changes on your object by refreshing it with the data from SimpleDB.

- **update**: This method will update the item by providing a Python dictionary with the attribute key/value pairs. You must once again call `save()` in order to persist the changes.

- **save**: This method will save the changes made to the item to SimpleDB by replacing the item in SimpleDB.

You can do all of these operations using boto as shown below:

```
>>> myitem1 = cars_domain.get_item('Car 1')
>>>
>>> myitem1.add_value('Model','530i')
>>>
>>> myitem1.save()
>>>
>>> myitem1.get('Model')
'530i'
>>>
>>> myitem1.has_key('Model')
True
>>>
>>> for i in myitem1.iterkeys():
...     print i
...
color
make
Model
>>>
>>> for i in myitem1.itervalues():
...     print i
...
Black
BMW
530i
>>>
>>> myitem1.keys()
[u'color', u'make', 'Model']
>>>
```

```
>>> myitem1.update({'Model':'X5'})
>>> myitem1.save()
>>>
>>> myitem1.values()
[u'Black', u'X5', u'BMW']
>>>
>>> myitem1.delete()
>>>
>>> myitem1.load()
>>>
>>> myitem1.values()
[]
>>>
```

Constraints on SimpleDB items

The constraints that you need to be aware of when working with SimpleDB items are:

- The length of the name for an item cannot be more than 1024 bytes.

- Each item can have a maximum 256 name/value pairs per item in a domain.

- The name of an item must only use characters that are UTF-8 characters, which are valid in XML documents. Control characters and any sequences that are not valid in XML are not allowed for use as part of an item name.

Attributes

Each item will have attributes, which are similar in concept to a column in a spreadsheet or a column in a database table. Each attribute is a key/value pair. The key is the unique name for the attribute and the value is the textual data for that key. SimpleDB is schemaless and allows you to have different attributes for each item in a domain. This is impossible in a relational database world where you must define your table schemas up front, and every time you need to add a new field or column, you must upgrade the schema for the database, or your existing applications might start throwing errors. SimpleDB frees you from this upgrade and maintenance cycle, and gives you the freedom to use this flexibility to your advantage when designing your applications.

If you add a new attribute to an item in a domain, only that item will have that attribute, and all the other existing items in the domain will hum along nicely without that additional attribute! You can see this in the following code samples.

Attributes with Java

Typica makes it really easy to add and manipulate the attributes of an item. The general pattern is to create a list of attributes and use the list to specify an item's attributes.

```java
SimpleDB sdb = new SimpleDB(awsAccessId, awsSecretKey, true);
try {
    Domain domain = sdb.getDomain("Cars");
    Item item = domain.getItem("Car 1");
    List<ItemAttribute> list = new ArrayList<ItemAttribute>();
    list.add(new ItemAttribute("make", "Mercedes", false));
    list.add(new ItemAttribute("color", "White", false));
    item.putAttributes(list);

    Item saved_item = domain.getItem("Car 1");
    for (ItemAttribute attr : saved_item.getAttributes()) {
        System.out.println("  " + attr.getName() + " = " + attr
            .getValue());
    }

    item = domain.getItem("Car 2");
    list = new ArrayList<ItemAttribute>();
    list.add(new ItemAttribute("make", "BMW", true));
    list.add(new ItemAttribute("color", "Black", true));
    item.putAttributes(list);

    saved_item = domain.getItem("Car 2");
    for (ItemAttribute attr : saved_item.getAttributes()) {
        System.out.println("  " + attr.getName() + " = " + attr
            .getValue());
    }

    item = domain.getItem("Car 1");
    list = new ArrayList<ItemAttribute>();
    list.add(new ItemAttribute("year", "2009", true));
    item.putAttributes(list);

    item = domain.getItem("Car 1");
    for (ItemAttribute attr : saved_item.getAttributes()) {
        System.out.println("  " + attr.getName() + " = " + attr
            .getValue());
    }
```

```
} catch (SDBException ex) {
    System.out.println(ex.getMessage());
}
```

Attributes with PHP

Consider the following PHP code sample:

```
$sdb = new SimpleDB(awsAccessKey, awsSecretKey); // create connection

$item_name = "car1";

// Add an attribute
$putAttributesRequest["make"] = array("value" => "BMW");
$putAttributesRequest["color"] = array("value" => "red");
$putAttributesRequest["year"] = array("value" => "2008");

// Replace existing values
$putAttributesRequest["desc"] = array("value" => "Sedan",
                                       "replace" => "true");

$putAttributesRequest["model"] = array("value" => "530i");

$sdb->putAttributes($domain,$item_name,$putAttributesRequest);
```

There are two examples of adding an attribute in this example. In the first example, we are adding a make of "BMW." In the second one, we are replacing a desc of "Sedan."

1. `$putAttributesRequest["make"] = array("value" => "BMW");`

   This line adds a single attribute/value pair.

   In this example, BMW will set as the value for make in item car1. Let's look at several possible situations.

Before	After (replace not specified)
No Make	Make = BMW for item car1
Make = BMW for item car1	Make = BMW for item car1 (no change)
Make = Mercedes for item car1	Make = Mercedes and Make = BMW for item car1

2. `$putAttributesRequest["desc"] = array("value" => "Sedan",`
   `                                       "replace" => "true");`

   The addition of the replace parameter set to true forces the current value(s) to be replaced with this value(s).

Before	After (replace=true)
No desc	desc=Sedan for item car1
desc=Sedan for item car1	desc=Sedan for item car1 (no change)
desc=SUV for item car1	desc=Sedan for item car1

Attributes with Python

Python code is a little more succinct, but follows a similar pattern for adding and modifying an item's attributes.

```
 >>> cars __domain.get_item('Car 1')
{u'color': u'White', u'make': u'Mercedes'}
>>>
>>> cars_domain.get_item('Car 2')
{u'color': u'Black', u'make': u'BMW'}
>>>
>>> myitem1 = cars_domain.get_item('Car 1')
>>> myitem1.add_value('year','2009')
>>> myitem1.save()
>>> myitem1
{u'color': u'White', u'make': u'Mercedes', 'year': '2009'}
>>> myitem2
{u'color': u'Black', u'make': u'BMW'}
>>>
```

Constraints on SimpleDB item attributes

Simple DB item attributes have the following constraints:

- The length of the name for an attribute cannot be more than 1024 bytes.
- The name of an attribute must only use characters that are UTF-8 characters, which are valid in XML documents. Control characters and any sequences that are not valid in XML are not allowed for use as part of an attribute name.

Values

Each attribute is a key/value pair, and the value is where you store the interesting stuff—your data! You can only store textual data in SimpleDB for now. There are some ways to get around it and store binary data in Amazon S3 and use metadata in SimpleDB to point to it. The only restriction textual data has, with a larger implication, is that you must encode and decode values for other data types such as dates and numbers when storing and retrieving them for use in your application.

One of the unique features of SimpleDB is the ability to have multiple values for a single attribute. These multiple values are actually stored by SimpleDB in such a way that you can query for each separately!

Storing multiple values in a single attribute with Java

You can store multiple values for an item by specifying the attribute multiple times with different values.

```java
SimpleDB sdb = new SimpleDB(awsAccessId, awsSecretKey, true);
try {
    Domain domain = sdb.getDomain("Cars");
    Item item = domain.getItem("Car 1");
    List<ItemAttribute> list = new ArrayList<ItemAttribute>();
    list.add(new ItemAttribute("dealer", "Tom the dealer", false));
    list.add(new ItemAttribute("dealer", "My local Mercedes",
        false));
    item.putAttributes(list);

    Item saved_item = domain.getItem("Car 1");
    for (ItemAttribute attr : saved_item.getAttributes()) {
        System.out.println("  " + attr.getName() + " = "
        + attr.getValue());
    }
} catch (SDBException ex) {
    System.out.println(ex.getMessage());
}
```

Storing multiple values in a single attribute with PHP

You can specify a multi-value value by assigning an array to the `value` such as in the `color` attribute line in the following code:

```
$sdb = new SimpleDB(awsAccessKey, awsSecretKey); // create connection

$item_name = "car1";

// Add an attribute
$putAttributesRequest["make"] = array("value" => "BMW");

// Add an attribute with multiple values
$putAttributesRequest["color"] =
    array("value" => array("grey","red"));
$putAttributesRequest["year"] = array("value" => "2008");

// Replace existing values
$putAttributesRequest["desc"] = array("value" => "Sedan",
    "replace" => "true");

$putAttributesRequest["model"] = array("value" => "530i");

print_r($sdb->
    putAttributes($domain,$item_name,$putAttributesRequest));
$putAttributesRequest["color"] =
    array("value" => array("grey","red"));
```

This line is adding two values to a single attribute. The result of this line depends on the original value of the attribute. The following table examines the before and after of this line.

Before	After (replace=true)
No color	color = grey and color = red for item car1
color = grey and color = red for item car1	color = grey and color = red for item car1
color = blue for item car1	color = blue and color = grey and color = red for item car1

Storing multiple values in a single attribute with Python

A single attribute in SimpleDB can have multiple values. In this section we will explore this feature using Python.

```
>>> myitem1.add_value('dealer','Tom the dealer, My local Mercedes')
>>>
>>> myitem1.save()
>>>
>>> myitem1
{u'color': u'White', u'make': u'Mercedes', 'dealer': 'Tom the dealer, My
local Mercedes', 'year': '2009'}
>>>
>>> myitem2.add_value('dealer','Tom the dealer')
>>>
>>> myitem2.save()
>>>
>>> myitem2
{u'color': u'Black', u'make': u'BMW', 'dealer': 'Tom the dealer'}
>>>
>>>
```

In this code sample, we added two different values for the `dealer` attribute.

You can store multiple values for an attribute by comma-separating the different values when adding or updating the attribute. Do not let the comma-separated values fool you into thinking that SimpleDB just stores the multiple values that way and you will need to do string parsing on your side while querying for matching values. SimpleDB actually stores and indexes these multiple values for the attribute in such a way as to make it very simple to query and retrieve them. They are stored conceptually as two different dealer attributes in our example data, but linked correctly with the right item.

The following figure gives a simple visualization of how multiple values are stored by SimpleDB internally. When you query for an attribute that has multiple values, the attribute is returned with multiple values that are comma-separated. However, internally SimpleDB stores the multiple values for an attribute as two similarly-named attributes with different values.

Name	Car 1
Make	Mercedes
Year	2009
Dealer	Tom the dealer
Dealer	My local Mercedes

Name	Car 1
Make	BMW
Dealer	Tom the dealer

Constraints on values of a SimpleDB item

A value stored in an attribute must follow these restrictions:

- The length of the value cannot be more than 1024 bytes.
- The value must only use characters that are UTF-8 characters, which are valid in XML documents. Control characters and any sequences that are not valid in XML are not allowed for use as part of the value. This is true for SOAP requests. Invalid XML characters inserted when using the REST API will be returned as base64-encoded values when retrieving an item later.

Consistent Read and Conditional Put / Delete announcement

Two key enhancements were announced on February 24, 2010 to SimpleDB: Consistent Read for `getAttributes`/Select and Conditional Put/Delete.

ConsistentRead = true for getAttributes and Select

Consistent Read enables you to get the most recent values bypassing the eventual consistency system. Consistent Read should not be used as a way to bypass eventual consistency, but is very useful in counters and code where reading the most recent value is critical.

In the following PHP sample, we create an item with the date/time and immediately use a getAttributes with ConsistentRead=true, then a normal getAttributes. The Consistent Read will return the just-updated value while the eventual consistency read will usually return the old value.

```php
$sdb = new SimpleDB(awsAccessKey, awsSecretKey);
  // create connection
$domain = "testread";
  // Check that the domain exists
$domainmd = $sdb->domainMetadata($domain);
echo("Domain $domain Metadata requested<br>");
echo("BoxUsage: ".$sdb->BoxUsage." = "
    . SimpleDB::displayUsage($sdb->BoxUsage)."<p>");

if (!$domainmd) { // Create if it does not exist
    if($sdb->createDomain($domain)) {
        echo("Domain $domain created<br>");
        echo("BoxUsage: ".$sdb->BoxUsage." = "
            . SimpleDB::displayUsage($sdb->BoxUsage)."<p>");
    }
}
// build array of items and attribute/value pairs
$putAttributesRequest = array();

$item_name = "testitem";
echo "putAttributes() record 'testitem'<br>";
$thetime = Time();  // get current time/date
$now = SimpleDB::encodeDateTime($thetime);
echo("ISO8601 format: $now &lt;-- NEW TIME<br>");

$putAttributesRequest["datetime"] =
    array("value" => $now, "replace" => "true");
  // store date time replace = true

// Put the latest date/time
$rest = $sdb->
    putAttributes($domain,$item_name,$putAttributesRequest);
if ($rest) {
    echo("Record $item_name created<br>");
    echo("BoxUsage: ".$sdb->BoxUsage." = "
        . SimpleDB::displayUsage($sdb->BoxUsage)."<br>");
} else {
    echo("Record $item_name FAILED<br>");
    echo("ErrorCode: ".$sdb->ErrorCode."<p>");
}

// Read back with ConsistentRead as true (fourth parameter)
$rest = $sdb->getAttributes($domain,$item_name,null,true);
```

```php
if ($rest) {
    echo "<br>getAttributes for $item_name ConsistentRead=True<br>";
    $datetime = $rest["datetime"];
    if ($now == $datetime) {
        echo "DateTime: $datetime &lt;-- NEW TIME<br>";
    } else {
        echo "DateTime: $datetime <b>&lt;-- OLD TIME </b><br>";
    }
    echo("BoxUsage: ".$sdb->BoxUsage." = "
        . SimpleDB::displayUsage($sdb->BoxUsage)."<br>");
} else {
    echo("Listing FAILED<br>");
    echo("ErrorCode: ".$sdb->ErrorCode."<p>");
}

// Normal eventual consistency read
$rest = $sdb->getAttributes($domain,$item_name);
if ($rest) {
    echo "<br>getAttributes for $item_name<br>";
    $now = $rest["datetime"];
    if ($thetime == $datetime) {
        echo "DateTime: $datetime &lt;-- NEW TIME<br>";
    } else {
        echo "DateTime: $datetime <b>&lt;-- OLD TIME </b><br>";
    }
    echo("BoxUsage: ".$sdb->BoxUsage." = "
        . SimpleDB::displayUsage($sdb->BoxUsage)."<br>");
} else {
    echo("Listing FAILED<br>");
    echo("ErrorCode: ".$sdb->ErrorCode."<p>");
}
```

The program when run returns:

```
putAttributes() record 'testitem'
ISO8601 format: 2010-02-27T20:01:09-04:00 <-- NEW TIME
Record testitem created
BoxUsage: 0.0000219909 = 22.0 muH

getAttributes for testitem ConsistentRead=True
DateTime: 2010-02-27T20:01:09-04:00 <-- NEW TIME
BoxUsage: 0.0000093222 = 9.3 muH

getAttributes for testitem
DateTime: 2010-02-27T20:01:09-04:00 <-- OLD TIME
BoxUsage: 0.0000093222 = 9.3 muH

    Domain: testread, item: testitem
```

In review, this program performed the following steps:

1. Set the `datetime` attribute to `2010-02-27T20:01:09-04:00`.

2. Read `datetime` using `getAttributes` with `ConsistentRead=true`.
   Returns `2010-02-27T20:01:09-04:00`.

3. Read `datetime` using `getAttributes`.
   Returns `2010-02-27T20:01:09-04:00 <-- OLD TIME`.

4. So using `ConsistentRead = true` with `getAttributes` and `Select` will return the most recent value bypassing eventual consistency.

Conditional Put / Delete

Conditional Put/Delete is being able to check for an existing condition before doing the put or delete. The check uses `ConsistentRead=true` so you are basing the decision on the most recent data.

Conditional Put allows you to add or replace one or more attributes to an item if the consistent value of a single-valued attribute has a specific value or does not exist. It is important to note that the condition is based on a single attribute value. It cannot be used with an attribute with multiple values. Conditional Delete is the same except you allow a delete rather than a put.

In this example, the program will fetch the attributes for a specific item `car3` and display them. Then it will try a delete with a condition that will fail, then a delete with a condition that will work.

```
$sdb = new SimpleDB(awsAccessKey, awsSecretKey);
  // create connection
$domain = "car-s";
$item_name = "car3";

$rest = $sdb->getAttributes($domain,$item_name);

if ($rest) {
    echo "<b>getAttributes for $item_name</b><pre>";
    print_r($rest);
    echo "</pre>";
    echo("RequestId: ".$sdb->RequestId."<br>");
    echo("BoxUsage: ".$sdb->BoxUsage." = " .
SimpleDB::displayUsage($sdb->BoxUsage)."<p>");
} else {
    echo("Listing FAILED<br>");
    echo("ErrorCode: ".$sdb->ErrorCode."<p>");
}
```

```
echo "<b>deleteAttributes item $item_name IF make =
    Acura (will fail)</b><pre>";
$putExists["make"] = array("value" => "Acura");
  // check if make = Acura
$rest=$sdb->deleteAttributes($domain,$item_name,null,$putExists);
  // delete whole record
if ($rest) {
    echo("Record $item_name updated<br>");
    echo("BoxUsage: ".$sdb->BoxUsage." = "
        . SimpleDB::displayUsage($sdb->BoxUsage)."<p>");
} else {
    echo("Record $item_name FAILED<br>");
    echo("ErrorCode: ".$sdb->ErrorCode."<p>");
}

unset($putExists);
echo "<b>deleteAttributes item $item_name
    IF make = Lexus (will succeed)</b><pre>";
$putExists["make"] = array("value" => "Lexus");
  // check if make = Acura
$rest=$sdb->deleteAttributes($domain,$item_name,null,$putExists);
  // delete whole record
if ($rest) {
    echo("Record $item_name updated<br>");
    echo("BoxUsage: ".$sdb->BoxUsage." = " .
SimpleDB::displayUsage($sdb->BoxUsage)."<p>");
} else {
    echo("Record $item_name FAILED<br>");
    echo("ErrorCode: ".$sdb->ErrorCode."<p>");
}
```

First, run seventh menu item (create multiple records with `batchPutAttributes` in `car-s`) to create the items.

The program when run returns:

```
getAttributes for car3
Array
(
    [color] => Array
        (
            [0] => Blue
            [1] => Red
        )

    [year] => 2008
```

```
        [make] => Lexus
)
RequestId: 16a1a20b-d42a-15d5-e002-33dc1197885e
BoxUsage: 0.0000093382 = 9.3 muH
deleteAttributes item car3 IF make = Acura (will fail)
Record car3 FAILED
ErrorCode: ConditionalCheckFailed
deleteAttributes item car3 IF make = Lexus (will succeed)
Record car3 updated
BoxUsage: 0.0000219907 = 22.0 muH
```

In review, the program did the following steps:

1. Fetch the attributes for item car3.

2. Delete car3 if make=Acura. As the make is Lexus this delete will fail.

3. Delete car3 if make=Lexus. This is the correct make so the item is deleted.

The expanded Java and Python APIs are not available as of the writing of the book. The concepts will be identical in those interfaces; the calls will just differ.

Summary

In this chapter, we discussed the SimpleDB model in detail. We explored the different methods for interacting with a domain, its items, and their attributes. We learned about the domain metadata. We also reviewed the various constraints imposed by SimpleDB on domains, items, and attributes.

Index

values 76
working 10
SimpleDB item attributes
constraints 75
SimpleDB items
constraints 72
constraints, on attributes 75
constraints, on values 79
SimpleDB service
AWS account 20
enabling, for AWS account 18, 20
SimpleDB, working
attributes 11
domain 10
item 10
values 11
SQL 51
strings 51
Structured Query Language. *See* **SQL**

T

Typica
batchPutAttributes method 58

deleteItem method 58
getItem method 58
getItemsAttributes method 58
getMetadata method 58
getName method 58
listItemsAttributes method 59
listItems method 58
listItemsWithAttributes method 59
methods 58
Typica library
about 23
downloading 28

V

values, SimpleDB
about 11, 76
constraints 79
multiple values storing in single attribute,
with Java 76
multiple values storing in single attribute,
with PHP 77
multiple values storing in single attribute,
with Python 78

Thank you for buying
Amazon SimpleDB: LITE

About Packt Publishing

Packt, pronounced 'packed', published its first book "Mastering phpMyAdmin for Effective MySQL Management" in April 2004 and subsequently continued to specialize in publishing highly focused books on specific technologies and solutions.

Our books and publications share the experiences of your fellow IT professionals in adapting and customizing today's systems, applications, and frameworks. Our solution based books give you the knowledge and power to customize the software and technologies you're using to get the job done. Packt books are more specific and less general than the IT books you have seen in the past. Our unique business model allows us to bring you more focused information, giving you more of what you need to know, and less of what you don't.

Packt is a modern, yet unique publishing company, which focuses on producing quality, cutting-edge books for communities of developers, administrators, and newbies alike. For more information, please visit our website: www.packtpub.com.

About Packt Enterprise

In 2010, Packt launched two new brands, Packt Enterprise and Packt Open Source, in order to continue its focus on specialization. This book is part of the Packt Enterprise brand, home to books published on enterprise software – software created by major vendors, including (but not limited to) IBM, Microsoft and Oracle, often for use in other corporations. Its titles will offer information relevant to a range of users of this software, including administrators, developers, architects, and end users.

Writing for Packt

We welcome all inquiries from people who are interested in authoring. Book proposals should be sent to author@packtpub.com. If your book idea is still at an early stage and you would like to discuss it first before writing a formal book proposal, contact us; one of our commissioning editors will get in touch with you.

We're not just looking for published authors; if you have strong technical skills but no writing experience, our experienced editors can help you develop a writing career, or simply get some additional reward for your expertise.

LITE Code: BS802NY3IY96

Amazon Web Services: Migrate your .NET Enterprise Application to the Amazon Cloud

ISBN: 978-1-84968-194-0   Paperback: 300 pages

Evaluate your Cloud requirements and successfully migrate your Enterprise .NET application to the AWS Platform

1. Get to grips with Amazon Web Services from a Microsoft Enterprise .NET viewpoint

2. Fully understand all of the AWS products including EC2, EBS, and S3

3. Quickly set up your account and manage application security

High Availability MySQL Cookbook

ISBN: 978-1-847199-94-2   Paperback: 264 pages

Over 60 simple but incredibly effective recipes focusing on different methods of achieving high availability for MySQL database

1. Analyze and learn different high availability options, including clustering and replication solutions within MySQL

2. Improve uptime of your MySQL databases with simple recipes showing powerful high availability techniques for MySQL

3. Tune your MySQL database for optimal performance.

Please check **www.PacktPub.com** for information on our titles

Oracle VM Manager 2.1.2

ISBN: 978-1-847197-12-2   Paperback: 244 pages

Manage a Flexible and Elastic Data Center with Oracle VM Manager

1. Learn quickly to install Oracle VM Manager and Oracle VM Servers

2. Learn to manage your Virtual Data Center using Oracle VM Manager

3. Import VMs from the Web, template, repositories, and other VM formats such as VMware

4. Learn powerful Xen Hypervisor utilities such as xm, xentop, and virsh

Oracle Coherence 3.5

ISBN: 978-1-847196-12-5   Paperback: 408 pages

Create Internet-scale applications using Oracle's high-performance data grid

1. Build scalable web sites and Enterprise applications using a market-leading data grid product

2. Design and implement your domain objects to work most effectively with Coherence and apply Domain Driven Designs (DDD) to Coherence applications

3. Leverage Coherence events and continuous queries to provide real-time updates to client applications

Please check **www.PacktPub.com** for information on our titles

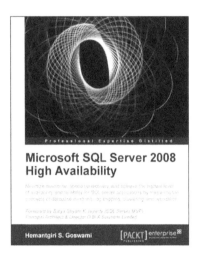

Microsoft SQL Server 2008 High Availability

ISBN: 978-1-84968-122-3   Paperback: 308 pages

Minimize downtime, speed up recovery, and achieve the highest level of availability and reliability for SQL server applications by mastering the concepts of database mirroring, log shipping, clustering, and replication

1. Install various SQL Server High Availability options in a step-by-step manner

2. A guide to SQL Server High Availability for DBA aspirants, proficient developers and system administrators

3. External references for further study

IBM WebSphere eXtreme Scale 6

ISBN: 978-1-847197-44-3   Paperback: 292 pages

Build scalable, high-performance software with IBM's data grid

1. Get hands-on experience with eXtreme Scale APIs, and understand the different approaches to using data grids

2. Introduction to new design patterns for both eXtreme Scale and data grids in general

3. Tutorial-style guide through the major data grid features and libraries

4. Start working with a data grid through code samples and clear walkthroughs

Please check **www.PacktPub.com** for information on our titles

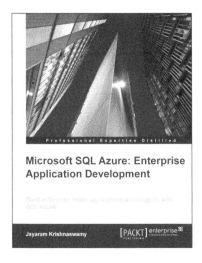
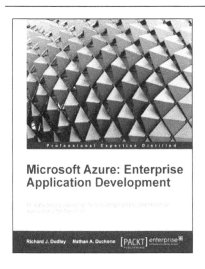

www.ingramcontent.com/pod-product-compliance
Lightning Source LLC
LaVergne TN
LVHW080101070326
832902LV00014B/2365